Foreword by
RICK FRISHMAN

I SEE YOUR NAME

EVERYWHERE

LEVERAGE THE POWER OF THE MEDIA
TO GROW YOUR FAME, WEALTH *and* SUCCESS

PAM LONTOS & ANDREA BRUNAIS

MORGAN JAMES PUBLISHING · NEW YORK

TABLE OF CONTENTS

TESTIMONIALS

These people know about the publicity expertise of Pam Lontos and Andrea Brunais. Read what they have to say about *I See Your Name Everywhere*!

"If you choose only one PR manual, make it *I See Your Name Everywhere* Here in one place are examples, tips and advice of immediate benefit to the reader. The authors offer potent self-promotion strategies, including a how-to section on crafting articles and getting them published in national journals and magazines."

Bob J. Danzig *Author, speaker & former CEO Hearst Newspapers*

* * * *

"Wow! This book tells you how to dramatically improve your image, credibility and market—faster and cheaper than you ever thought possible."

Brian Tracy *Author, The Psychology of Selling*

* * * *

"This is the best collection of publicity tactics ever assembled. I owe three best-selling books to doing what they told me to do. If you want to stand out from the competition and see your name everywhere, do what they tell you to do!"

Jason Jennings *New York Times best-selling author, It's Not the Big that Eat the Small—It's the Fast that Eat the Slow, Less is More and Think BIG—Act Small*

* * * *

"This is a terrific book written in an easy-to-read style that offers a clear explanation of media and publicity. It's a must-read for any small business owner."

Jerry D. Simmons *Former vice president, director of field sales, Time Warner Book Group, and author, What Writers Need to Know About Publishing*

"Pam Lontos' experience in sales, marketing and public relations, along with her media savvy, can jump-start your career."

Zig Ziglar

* * * *

"The techniques in *I See Your Name Everywhere* were a major factor in taking a $10-an-hour no-name Nebraska farm girl and a nonexistent industry to an international training program for Paper Tiger Authorized Consultants in an organizing industry which now includes magazines, TV shows, and a national association with 4000-plus members."

Barbara Hemphill, *Author, Taming the Paper Tiger*

* * * *

"If there is one book that accurately defines precise publicity tactics, it's *I See Your Name Everywhere.* This comprehensive guide provides the tips and tools to get the publicity that will set you apart from the competition."

Dan Poynter, *author, The Self-Publishing Manual*

* * * *

"*I See Your Name Everywhere* is among the most informative and practical how-to guides on implementing successful publicity tactics. It should be considered required reading for anyone who wants to advance his or her publishing career."

Brian Jud, *author, How to Make Real Money Selling Books*

* * * *

"This guide to successful publicity tactics is a must for those who want more for themselves and their company. Well-organized and to the point, comprehensive and yet concise enough to use daily, *I See Your Name Everywhere* offers valuable insights on getting media coverage. I have always wanted to know how my PR firm got my name seen everywhere — now Pam and Andrea tell us all!"

Dr. Maurice Ramirez, *president, High Alert, LLC*

"I attribute the effective use of well-placed PR to much of my success. I have never recommended a book with this level of excitement! *I See Your Name Everywhere* is a keeper!"

Sy Sperling, *founder, Hair Club for Men*

* * * *

"In a competitive market, leveraging the power of the media is crucial. Getting noticed is key to creating fame, wealth and success. PR guru Pam Lontos and journalist Andrea Brunais, teaming up, have created a guide that offers a roadmap for getting into the media."

Gene Perret, *comedy writer for Bob Hope*

* * * *

"I love the title for this book. It describes the perfect result of a well-executed PR campaign: *I See Your Name Everywhere.* If you want to hear that statement attached to your PR campaign, this book is a must-read. I expect to see its name everywhere very soon."

John Kremer, *author, 1001 Ways to Market Your Books, and webmaster, BookMarket.com*

* * * *

"This dynamic book provides insider secrets for lasting success in the media. Every business leader, author and speaker needs *I See Your Name Everywhere* in their library. It's truly a must have!"

Dick Bruso, *branding expert and founder, Heard Above The Noise*

* * * *

"The secret to generating publicity is not simply reaching reporters and editors, it's understanding their language and how they think. This book is a vital resource full of ideas and strategies on how to market yourself to the press and other news media. It will guide you on how to create that buzz. If you want to stand out in your community, attract national attention and uniquely position yourself in the eyes of the media, this is a must-have reference book. Buy a copy, change how others see you, get the attention you deserve."

Brian J. Bieler, *former president, Viacom Radio Group, and author, The Sales Operator — Insider's Guide to Successful Selling*

* * * *

"Finally, a no-nonsense guidebook for publicity! Andrea's expertise flows from every page of this book. Once I started reading it, I knew I had found the answers for all my future media needs."

Kendra Trahan, *author and publisher, Disneyland Detective and Disney's California Detective*

* * * *

"Pam Lontos is a public-relations dynamo! Her persistence and skill have gotten clients coverage in the nation's top print and electronic media, from *NBC News* to *Business Week*, *Time* magazine and beyond. The stories she shares help make this book a must read!"

Cord Cooper, *national newspaper columnist*

* * * *

"Pam Lontos and Andrea Brunais have written an engaging, conversational book, and one that's indispensable, I would think, for anyone who wants to get a handle on public relations and what type of stories interest reporters. And I would know. I've been quoting Pam's clients in numerous articles for over 10 years."

Geoff Williams, *freelance journalist and frequent contributor to Entrepreneur magazine*

* * * *

"When Pam Lontos writes about media relations and publicity, I pay attention. This new book is a must-read for anyone in business, sports, politics, or other field in the public arena. Lots of good practical lessons to put into action."

Pat Williams, *senior vice president, Orlando Magic*

"Finally, a book that gets it right! *I See Your Name Everywhere* provides a unique combination of to-the-point publicity techniques, valuable tips and advice from seasoned experts."

Irwin Zucker, *founder and president, Emeritus, Book Publicists of Southern California, and president, Promotion in Motion*

* * * *

"Today publicity is an overwhelmingly powerful force. Pam and Andrea really know PR! I recommend that you read *I See Your Name Everywhere* It contains all the elements any individual or business needs to know to use the power of the media to get them to the top of their game!"

Jim Cathcart, *author, How to Create & Grow High-Value Relationships*

FOREWORD

BY
RICK FRISHMAN

Today more than any time in history, entrepreneurs and professionals compete in saturated marketplaces. They must find ways to distinguish themselves. Successful people attract clients and customers by not only claiming competence, but also by demonstrating authority. There is no greater way to display credentials and prove expertise than to become someone the news media repeatedly consults, publishes and quotes.

How to become that authoritative source? You can sit around lamenting the fact that you possess more knowledge and experience than your competitors and yet their profiles are higher than yours. Or you can develop a skill set that will empower you to approach reporters and editors confident that they will receive your pitches enthusiastically, print your bylined articles and quote you in their stories.

How is this possible? Print, TV, Internet, and radio journalists all require content. Reporters and editors behave in predictable ways as they go about gathering and preparing that content. *I See Your Name Everywhere* shares the principles that underlie this process. Better yet, it details specific ways to go about earning the news coverage you deserve.

Forget about spin. Reporters and editors are allergic to spin! First you must make yourself ready for media coverage by combining an understanding of news value with your ability to offer something unique. Then you are ready for seasoned professionals Pam Lontos and Andrea Brunais to teach you to see opportunity—to tell your own story. Armed with a plan of attack, you can approach the news media effectively by knowing how editors think and understanding the etiquette of making the approach.

Pam Lontos has achieved extraordinary results in her firm PR/PR, with her clients regularly showing up in premier magazines and newspapers including the *Wall Street Journal, The New York Times* and *USA Today* as well as on national television. Andrea Brunais knows journalism inside and out, winning awards such as the national Robert Kennedy reporting award and, switching to the PR field, more than doubling positive publicity for a major cancer and research institute.

I See Your Name Everywhere is necessary reading for everyone who wants to stand out in the crowd, achieve recognition for expertise and reach literally millions of potential consumers. *I See Your Name Everywhere* allows readers to gain insights based on Lontos' and Brunais' professional experience and to follow step-by-step instructions leading to success.

More comprehensive than the typical PR advice book, *I See Your Name Everywhere* offers how-to lessons not just at the primary level of writing a news release but also in the more advanced arena of setting up news conferences, preparing for interviews and landing guest spots on TV and radio news shows. A look at the table of contents shows plenty of proven tactics and techniques to generate publicity using the free media. But complementing that fun subject area is a serious addressing of crisis communications—a subject every business or organization, no matter its size, must be prepared to handle.

With a little bit of newsworthiness and a lot of expertise, you can be on your way. You can be quoted in magazines and newspapers. You can give sound bites or in-depth interviews on TV and radio programs. You can write articles and opinion pieces published under your name. This helpful book shows you how to accomplish all of the above and more. I have been a professional for more than 31 years, and there is no better guide to understanding the tremendous power of the news media with instructions for how you can harness it.

Rick Frishman
Author, WHERE'S YOUR WOW: 16 Ways to Get Your Competitors to Wish They Were You
www.rickfrishman.com

CHAPTER ONE

UNDERSTANDING MEDIA RELATIONS: THE BASICS OF FAME-BUILDING

CHAPTER 1:
Understanding Media Relations:
The Basics of Fame-Building

Become media savvy, and you can grow your wealth, fame and success. Publicity can come from anywhere and in many different forms. It can be as simple as having a letter published on the opinion pages of your local newspaper or as mind-blowing as a front page interview in *The Wall Street Journal* or an appearance on *Oprah*.

What's more, today's traditional news media compete alongside new forms of outreaching including blogs and podcasts. Authors, speakers and entrepreneurs must earn mentions in the news media—both traditional and new—if their businesses are to survive and flourish. Media coverage translates into instant credibility.

Generating publicity is a learned art. We are practitioners of that art. In this book, we will share our decades of experience in the PR and news-media worlds, helping people eager to advance their personal or professional interests. The same news-generating principles apply whether you are a CEO, entrepreneur, doctor, lawyer, nonprofit executive, professional speaker or book author.

Anyone can have his or her 15 minutes of fame, as Andy Warhol famously predicted. But it takes knowledge and persistence to leverage that 15 minutes into long-term media exposure. You want to become a trusted source journalists turn to time after time. Just look at the disparate types of people we have helped launched into the national spotlight:

- A former Bell South executive who teaches people to organize their paperwork

- A medical doctor who prays with his patients

- The author of a novel whose work is now being made into a movie starring James Garner

- A comedian who gives corporate workshops on humor

- A teenager who discovered a cancer-preventing property in red wine

- A businessman who sells voice-recognition products to companies

All of these people were quoted in national publications including *Time, Investor's Business Daily, Reader's Digest, the Wall Street Journal* and *USA Today.*

Media coverage can open doors, increase your speaking fees, connect you with new markets and take your career or business to the next level. Pamela Harper, president of the corporate-strategy consulting company Business Advancement, was getting nowhere as she attempted to snag a speaking engagement with a high-powered convention of executives. There was no budget for a speaker for the next convention, the bored-sounding meeting planner on the other end of the line told her. No money for hotel, either. Then Harper asked,

"Do you have a copy of *Executive Talent* on your desk?" The meeting planner did. "Open it—I'm in there!" Sure enough, the article featuring Harper was enough to dazzle the meeting planner. Harper soon had her contract in hand—at her named fee.

Also a case in point: Sy Sperling, founder of the Hair Club for Men. When Sperling decided he wanted a second career as a business and motivational speaker, he began writing articles such as "Marketing on a Shoestring" for trade publications. His exposure? More than 35 national magazines in one month.

You can be your own publicist by becoming a recognized expert source the news media will return to time after time. You can reach new markets by enlarging your presence in the "free media."

Paid advertising, on the other hand, is becoming more expensive every day. To buy a full-page ad that runs just once in *Oprah* magazine costs more than $100,000, in the *New York Times* almost $150,000, and in *Parade* magazine more than $600,000. Such an ad even in your local major metropolitan daily will cost almost six figures; for example, the *Dallas Morning News* ad rate for a full-page ad is $94,691.

The cost of paid coverage is high. Ironically, people are less likely to believe what they read in this advertisement that has cost you dearly. However, when it comes to earning "free media" coverage, the stakes are high. You're competing against all those other people who want to become famous or drive business to their enterprises.

Desire for fame is ingrained in our culture. It is a given.

Journalist Bill Moyers once interviewed the late Joseph Campbell, comparative mythologist and author, saying, "We seem to worship celebrities today, not heroes."

"Yes, and that's too bad," Campbell agreed. "A questionnaire was once sent around one of the high schools in Brooklyn which asked, 'What would you like to be?' Two thirds of the students responded, 'A celebrity.' They had no notion of having to give of themselves in order to achieve something."

Today, more than 20 years later, the Pew Research Center documented that same overarching desire among American young people. Eighty-one percent of 18 to 25-year-olds said getting rich is their generation's most important or second-most-important life goal, while 51 percent gave the answer 'being famous.' Reporting on the poll results, *USA Today* quoted David Morrison of the Philadelphia-based research firm Twentysomething Inc.: "People being themselves can be incredibly famous and get sponsorship deals, and they can become celebrities."

Fame is not only the means to promote one's products or business but also an end in itself.

Trick of the trade: Whether you do radio, television or print, or a combination thereof, the key is to focus on the media that reaches the audience you want and delivers the results you need. Decide if you're trying to build credibility, raise your speaking fees or sell more products. Decide on whether you're trying to reach the masses— whether they are decision-makers or not. Are you selling expensive services or an inexpensive product? Your goals will determine the media that is right for you.

When starting your public relations campaign, you must decide where to put your emphasis. You want to target your writing or your interview quotes or soundbites to the right people by using the right kind of medium. So how do you decide whether to do print, television or radio? (We will deal with blogs and podcasts in a later chapter.)

There are certainly advantages for each medium, but you want to target your public relations campaign to what is best for your goals. You must also consider what it is you are selling—is it an expensive service that only a targeted group would want? Or is it a relatively inexpensive product such as a book or CD that would be good for the masses?

Here are some questions to ask that can help you decide which media is right for your publicity campaign:

1. **Do you want businesses to hire you?** Do you have a service that professionals would want? Then print is a great choice for you. You can target the right audience by focusing on some of the many different publications out there—there is one for each industry, hobby, organization and interest. From women's magazines to business magazines, newsstand publications such as *Inc.* or *Cosmopolitan* to industry publications like real estate or financial magazines, there are a variety of ways to target a specific audience. In addition, studies have shown that print builds up your name and credibility more than any other medium because it is viewed as more reliable and believable than television or radio.

2. **Is your goal to build credibility?** Are you interested in a long-term impact? Do you want to increase your bookings or fees? If so, print is a good option. People believe more in print than anything they hear on the radio or see on television. For example, many radio stations announced

that Lisa Marie Presley married Michael Jackson, but audiences didn't believe it when they heard it. Later that night, television shows picked up the story and announced the same thing, but audiences who saw it thought it was just a rumor. Finally, when the story was published in print, people believed it. Print gives you credibility, whether you are a writer talking about your book in *Cosmopolitan* or a featured author in an industry publication like *Real Estate Professional* or *Credit Union Magazine*. The audience assumes that when they see your name in print, you are the expert or leading authority on the topic. Print also helps build a long-term exposure because people keep magazines for months, even years, often sharing their favorite articles with friends, colleagues and family members. In fact, one speaker received a call for a speaking engagement with a major corporation after they read his article—even though the article was published 10 years earlier.

3. **Are you selling to the masses?** Is your product or service economical enough that everyone can afford it? If so, radio is a great option. Radio targets the masses— after all, everyone has access to a radio, whether they are soccer moms, business executives, students or taxi drivers. You can even target specific groups. For instance, if your product is featured during the morning rush hour, you'll likely be reaching businesspeople on their way to work, as well as students and parents driving to school. Also, you can choose a specific radio station or show that targets a specialized market, such an afternoon talk show that attracts young men age 18-25 or a local show that reaches two or three counties in the area. This medium is not as good for getting more speaking engagements or raising

your fees because you are reaching many people who may not all need your product or service. However, if you have a product intended for the masses, it is a great medium. Also, keep in mind that after being on a radio show you will see fast results within the hour, but then it's gone until the next time you come on. If you're selling a book on the radio, you'll want to be sure that it's out and widely available at bookstores or online.

4. **Is your product or service available nationwide?** Is it something that would appeal to the masses? If so, then television is a good choice for you. Similar to radio, you can reach the masses and also have the option of targeting your message to a specific audience. With television, you have the flexibility of targeting a certain area, by choosing a local station or show. You can also target a specific audience—such as 25 to 45-year-olds that watch the cooking channel or teens and young adults who watch the MTV network. Like radio, you can experience fast sales in just a few hours, but then it will stop unless you are booked on the show regularly and frequently. Be sure that before you are booked on the television show, your product is fully stocked and available in stores or online; otherwise you'll be missing out on sales.

Quick quiz for deciding how to start building your media strategy

Many people in the community:
A. may have heard of my company
B. are familiar with my company and have a good impression of it
C. probably have a negative view of my company because of previous media coverage

If my company showed up in the headlines:
A. people would wonder why such an unknown entity would rate news coverage
B. my company would likely be portrayed in a positive light
C. my day would probably be ruined

If a reporter called, my reaction would be one of:
A. surprise and slight nervousness; the situation is relatively new to me
B. pleasure; it's about time they wrote about my company again
C. caution or wariness; reporters are prone to inaccuracies and misquotes

My company scrapbook over the past five years:
A. probably has one or two newspaper clippings
B. consists of more than one volume, tabbed and labeled
C. is something I would rather not pull out to be reminded of troubled times

News coverage about my company:
A. is so skimpy I can't characterize it
B. portrays my company and its mission fairly accurately

C. creates misimpressions with the public and is filled with mistakes

How many reporters do you personally know and what is your relationship with them?
A. I don't know any
B. one or two; I see them a couple of times a year
C. there's one reporter I respect, but if I never saw most of the SOBs again, that would be fine with me

If you answered mostly A, you probably need to pay closest attention to the chapters on scoring positive publicity and interviewing. You need, first, to understand the media and then to put an effective outreach strategy into place to build public awareness and support for your mission. If you answered mostly B, concentrate on building relationships with reporters. Consider some advanced means for generating news coverage, such as writing op-ed pieces or holding a news conference. If your answers fell mostly into the C range, focus on crisis communications and consider investing in media training for yourself or your organization.

CHAPTER TWO

WHAT DRIVES NEWS REPORTERS

At the end of the day, the story is turned in and judged against every other reporter's story. The best story becomes "lead" news. In newspapers, that means it is placed on the front page of the paper or, second best, on the front page of the local section. In the television lineup, the lead story comes first. The difference between the criteria that newspapers use to select their best story and that of TV is summed up in an amusingly cynical phrase that describes television news: "if it bleeds, it leads." Turn on your local TV news and, if there has been a homicide or gory traffic accident that day, the news anchors will tell you about it before they turn to any other happenings.

So what makes a compelling story? The No. 1 aspect of a compelling story has not changed since the days the founders wrote the First Amendment:

Conflict.

Every story has conflict. Don't kid yourself that it doesn't. Even feature stories contain conflict. Even mass-appeal Oprah themes embody conflict.

In March 2007 Oprah presented an emotion-filled, touching guest in Isaiah Kacyvenski—Rams linebacker, Super Bowl star, full-scholarship Harvard grad. He grew up in ghastly conditions: poor, at times homeless, all the while physically abused by his alcoholic dad. His mom died the day of his first major game. The dad, a recovering alcoholic, sat in the audience's front row. Conflict? You bet. It was Isaiah against his dad (now reconciled), Isaiah against poverty, Isaiah against the world. How this sweet man, who keeps the Isaiah Bible verse his mom highlighted posted in his locker, overcame those odds could make even a veteran news reporter cry.

The more sharply the reporter can draw the conflict, the greater the chance the editors will choose his or her story as that day's lead.

Disagreement, competing values, charges and accusations—all spell conflict. Two of the clients of PR/PR ended up quoted in the same story on the front page of *USA Today*. Each took a totally different tack in commenting on Circuit City's firing of 3,400 workers, simultaneously announcing plans to replace them with lower-paid staff. Maryland-based business consultant Francie Dalton justified the act as a smart business move, while Paul Endress of Pennsylvania, whose company teaches psychological principles in hiring and keeping workers, spoke to the need to reassure the remaining workers that the company was stronger and they were safe. A third expert played up the poor morale likely to plague the survivors of the layoff. Notice how the reporter employed each expert's quotes to define, sharpen and intensify the conflict, thereby inviting her editors to give the story Page 1-A play.

Trick of the trade: No matter how curious you are, never ask a reporter to show you the story before it goes on the air or in print. Not only will you look like a novice, but also you may actually offend the reporter. At some newspapers and magazines, a reporter could be fired for showing you the story in advance because this would indicate a greater allegiance to one person quoted in the story than to another. Or a greater allegiance to a source than to "the truth." You sometimes can get away with asking to read certain technical paragraphs of a story to check for accuracy. In that case, confine your comments to the facts, not the reporter's approach. The press values its independence.

Reporters have only a few hours to piece their stories together. Sometimes they have only a few minutes. The news cycle these days is 24/7. The vast majority of reporters are not interested in making you look bad. They are interested in, primarily, accuracy and, secondarily, truth. (If you have questions about the difference, take another look at the old Sally Field movie *Absence of Malice*.) They must gather and cross-check their facts, racing against time and their competitors.

We have already established that the reporter's desire for that day is to have his or her story chosen for the lead. But what are a reporter's dreams? All reporters want their stories to be so good that they are repeatedly chosen to lead the newspaper's front page or the news station's daily broadcast. They want their writing to be so vivid that their colleagues are envious. They want their facts to be so well marshaled that their editors don't bother to pepper them with questions or try to poke holes in their story, because the reporter has trained the editor to expect airtight work.

In addition, they want the stories they work on to be judged of compelling public importance so that they might win state and national journalism awards, which also increase reporters' status within the profession.

Reporters who perform outstandingly and who are consistent in their output can better control their career paths. If they desire to be promoted to editor, this will happen sooner rather than later. If they want to move to a bigger market or a newspaper with a grand reputation, they do it by delivering the goods day after day.

The fear, conversely, is that they will make a mistake or that they will commit something false to the airwaves or to print. Human beings make mistakes, and reporters are no exception, especially in long stories where many sets of facts and perspectives come into play. Errors are inevitable. The reporter can only hope to do his or her best to be fair, to render faithfully what sources have said and to paint an accurate picture of the conflict that is inevitably present (or there would be no story).

The reporter's worst fear is that he or she will make an error so big that his or her career ends on account of sloppy reporting or someone files a lawsuit against the newspaper. Lawsuits aren't always bad news to the reporter because parties can file them out of anger at being portrayed in an unflattering light. If the reporter's story is accurate, he or she has little to worry about. So reporters may ask questions over and over or ask for documents to substantiate what you are saying. This is their job.

Once you know this, if you are the target of a news story, what may seem as the reporter's Columbo-like pursuit of you will seem less intimidating. Reporters will always try to gain backup for what you are saying from a second or a third source. Unverified information can put their careers at risk. Consider Judith Miller at *The New York Times*. Many of her former colleagues have an entirely different view of her now that facts have become clear that she swallowed uncritically the Bush administration's line that stockpiled weapons of mass destruction existed in Iraq.

Why should you care what motivates reporters?

They will tell your story to the public. The public is more likely to believe them than to believe information from other sources, including information coming directly from you or your organization. The informed public is several times more likely to believe information in articles or news coverage than material in corporate or product advertising, surveys of U.S. and European opinion leaders.

News about you and your company touches far more people than you can interact with personally. News reporting can make your community and constituents look askance at you. News reporting can even bring prosecutors knocking at your door. On the flip side, news reporting can bolster your reputation in a way that makes advancing your mission easier. News reporting can position you as an expert, help you reach new markets, help you succeed in both your personal and professional goals.

What constitutes a juicy story?

In seeking positive publicity for yourself, your book or your business, you need to understand the triggers. Certain factors will generate reporter interest:

- Involvement of money

- Trend stories

- Scientific breakthroughs and disease cures

- Corruption

- A yearly anniversary date of a big story or crime.

Here are some factors that make a story bigger:

- Timeliness

- Proximity (closeness to home)

- Nature and severity of the conflict

- Celebrity

- Size of the impact once the story plays out

- Human interest level, sometimes called "color"

How competition among media outlets affects you.

Because reporters are working at a pace unheard-of before the age of the Internet, the need for speed has created new urgency in the reporter's workday. No longer are there days and hours to put together a story. To be first on the air, on the street or on the Web, the reporter must collect facts *now*. Five minutes from now can be too late to respond to a reporter; he or she may be on the line with another source by the time you get around to calling back. Reporters simply will not wait.

From a story-pitching point of view, waiting too long can kill your chances of being quoted in a national publication. One of the clients of PR/PR—an expert in profiling serial killers—thought about it for 48 hours after a gruesome crime that was reported nationally, coming up with an angle to speak about and letting reporters know of his availability. The answers came back: it's too late. Call us on the *same day* next time there's a massacre.

Some strategies for dealing with reporters.

Now that you know the basics of a news reporter's motivations, here are some tactics for cultivating the news media.

Reporters are human. Many prefer to deal with someone they know than to make a cold call. If the local reporters who cover your area or industry have not contacted you, reach out to them. You can say you simply want to get to know them should a situation arise where they are covering you on deadline. If you are important to a reporter's area of coverage, you might invite them for a field trip or tour. If you are a small player, offer to meet them for coffee in a location near the newsroom. That way the reporter has the benefits of a face-to-face meeting with a potential source without too much time invested.

If you make a phone call to the reporter to set this up, speak crisply in a businesslike way and get right to the point. Do not call when they are on deadline. Late afternoon is a terrible time to call a daily newspaper's reporter or editor. Likewise, don't call a noon anchor at 11:30 a.m. Reporters' phones ring off the hook. Many reporters, even at medium-sized newspapers, receive upwards of 400 e-mails per day, and phones ring constantly.

The goal is to create a relationship. A reporter who knows and likes you will not relish skewering you in print or on the air. Also, a familiar give-and-take of information will increase the chances that you will be called upon to provide information when a deadline story occurs—which is exactly what you want. When you are quoted repeatedly in your field, you are building credibility. You create that sought-after top-of-mind awareness.

Whenever you are talking to a reporter, remember that everything you say is "on the record." That means any of your words could conceivably end up in a news story. Do not say anything you would not be comfortable having immortalized in print or pixels. Reporters won't put words in your mouth, although they may well tighten up your thoughts, so don't say anything that isn't clear and concise. Be especially careful when a reporter tells you negative information someone else has supposedly said. Be careful how you correct unfair or false information; you can end up quoted in a way that breeds enmity and prolongs misunderstandings in your industry or field.

At the same time, don't be so uptight that the reporter cannot take some pleasure in your presence or conversation. Relationships build when you can interact with a reporter in a mutually enjoyable way. At the H. Lee Moffitt Cancer Center & Research Institute, the chief of research was always getting his wings clipped by the administration for supposedly saying too much, too casually to the news media. One of his phrases was taken as an insult to the affiliated university next door, for instance. Another time he blew the lid off the capital campaign, which was not supposed to be announced for another three months. But the news media loves this white-haired, brilliant "mad scientist," in part because of his wacky sense of humor. Halfway through an interview with Howard Troxler, top columnist for the *St. Petersburg Times*, Troxler grinned, reached across the desk to shake Dr. Jack Pledger's hand and said, "I like you!" Getting that sort of reaction from a journalist is akin to wringing a compliment out of American Idol's Simon

Cowell. If your organization has a maverick the news media like, count yourself lucky.

When you are networking with reporters, don't always be focused on your self-interested goal of generating good publicity for you or your company. You wouldn't want to be labeled a "user" in your social or business relationships; the same holds true in the media world. From time to time, contact a journalist you know just because. You can write them a congratulatory note about a story they wrote that you admired. You can introduce them to a source they have been trying to meet, perhaps even someone in an industry outside of yours. You can also give them leads and tips that might result in a good story that doesn't involve your company in any way.

Major distinctions between print and TV reporters.

Reporters from broadcast and print media are equally motivated by the daily desire to make a big splash. That being said, key differences exist.

The print reporter may hang around for a long time, asking question after question and seeking many people to talk to. The TV reporter may buzz quickly in and out, recording a soundbite from a key member of your organization before rushing off.

The print reporter may ask for documents, articles and printouts of e-mails. The TV reporter will probably ask for "visuals"— a picture of something to illustrate the topic or a "B-roll" shot of people at work to run silently behind a voiceover.

The print reporter may seem devoted to dissecting the nuances of the subject matter. By contrast, the TV crew may be more concerned about the practicalities of lighting and places to plug in their equipment.

The print reporter will want you to speak slowly enough for note taking. TV people prefer crisp, smooth soundbites. If the journalists like you, they will continue to want to work with you. No matter who they work *for*, whether broadcast or print, they will not forget when you make their jobs easier or harder.

Checklist for responding effectively to reporters.

When a story is in progress:

- work to get the information requested as soon as possible

- think what visuals you or your organization might provide to a TV reporter

- prepare a one-page list of bullet points to help the reporter better understand the story

- e-mail the reporter the correct spellings of all the names and titles of people interviewed from your organization

- always remember that everything you say is "on the record" unless you both formally agree otherwise in advance, and even then be careful

Between stories if there is a regular reporter on your beat:

- keep a list of their preferred methods of contact and the story types that most interest them

- call to give them a lead on a story unrelated to your organization so they know you are interested in them and not just what they can do for you

- follow their work so you know what they have been covering and send them feedback from time to time

- never give gifts, but unless their employer has a strict policy against it, treat them to coffee or lunch once in a while and allow them to reciprocate

CHAPTER THREE

WRITING FOR THE NEWS MEDIA

CHAPTER 3:
Writing for the News Media

Authoring your own articles is a great way to achieve media coverage. On the opinion pages, the op-ed article written by an expert is a staple. The feature pages are filled with columnists—genealogy, antiques, relationships, pets, real estate and other topics. For small weekly newspapers, which are well read in their communities, you may be able to write original news stories that will be published verbatim. *Newsweek* runs its venerable "My Turn" column, and National Public Radio has resurrected the guest-authored "This I Believe" essay.

As you decide what to write about, teach yourself to think in terms of headlines. Refine your message in anticipation of the day you will write something or your organization will become part of the news. First you must create in yourself the constant awareness of the information—what PR consultants call "key messages"—that you most want the public to know about you and your business.

To start, remember that information comes at people all day long. Thousands of commercial messages, hundreds of news items and scores of work-related directives bombard us. And that's not even counting *personal* e-mails and phone calls. Here's where to start: In concert with your colleagues or communication professionals, in-house or otherwise, decide the most important message you want a reader or viewer to remember about your company. Use commutes, line waiting and other downtime to think of new ways to convey these messages at every opportunity.

Even when you are simply contacting a journalist, you will need to write. Because so many journalists work under almost inhuman time constraints, they are not fond of telephone contact. Phone calls eat up time that could be devoted to research, writing, thinking or dealing with the aftermath of yesterday's story. Reporters and editors sometimes act as if they are allergic to phone calls, because predictably the person on the other end of the line is out in the "real world" working on "normal time" that does not apply to the hectic, frenzied pace at which journalists must feed the daily maw.

Therefore much of your communication with the news media will be written, whether it is delivered via fax, e-mail or snail mail or even hand-delivered. If you understand the protocol, you will increase the chances of achieving the desired response or result.

You can send story ideas in writing, for instance, hoping to catch the interest of a writer or editor. The basic means of conducting media relations—the news release—is a form of written communication. Letters to the editor and op-ed pieces will have no chance of being published if they do not conform to rules of good writing in the style of the news media.

You may also wish to contact a reporter or editor (and in extreme cases, his or her bosses) in writing if a story about you or your company contained errors of fact. In most cases, you will want to let small things slide in the interests of maintaining a good working relationship if the reporter has acted in good faith. However, in some cases, allowing misrepresentations to enter the media's archives is too potentially damaging because mistakes are repeated when reporters in the future draw from those archives.

If you lack the time, inclination or capability to write for the media on your own, you might wish to hire a media-relations expert to produce this work for you. Surveys of independent practitioners show the rates charged currently average from $80 to $120 per hour. Agency rates are higher, although you don't see the per-hour charge because you generally pay by the project. Work coming from independent practitioners can be of equal or even higher quality.

> **Trick of the trade:** When sending e-mail, write a subject line that contains your name, your institution's or business's name and the type of e-mail you are sending. A subject line packed with information designed to appeal to the recipient will help get your e-mails read. Always put your text in the body of the e-mail, *never* as an attachment, unless asked. Attachments may trigger a media outlet's spam filter, and in any event journalists almost never open the attachment (unless they personally asked you to send it).

News release. As outlined in previous chapters, journalists resent being forced to read a news release several times to extract its news value. Think through your story and place the most compelling, unique or new aspect in the lead paragraph.

A news release is set up as follows:

NEWS RELEASE
contact information for media relations staff
include phone and e-mail

ATTENTION: news editors, science editors (or any relevant editors) Photographs available

1 to 2-LINE HEADLINE

YOUR CITY NAME—(date of the news release) text begins here and takes up no more than a page.

"A quote from the CEO or appropriate staff member can be the third or fourth paragraph."

You can fill in more details here, but don't let the news release run more than one page, double or 1.5 line spaced.

End with a single-spaced, italicized paragraph of boilerplate information about your company.

Media advisory. A media advisory draws from the day's news and "localizes" it to you, your company, or your institution. Set up as above, but say "media advisory" instead of "news release."

In the first sentence, summarize the day's news. In the second, why you think your organization ties into this news. For instance: "The U.S. Food and Drug Administration has seized thousands of morphine pain pumps from warehouses across the country, claiming shoddy workmanship by the manufacturer, Company X.

"Dr. No-Pain Pang of My Institution has been studying Company X's pain pump for the last 18 months and has previously published a journal article on pain pumps. He is available for interviews...."

Pitch. The story pitch is similar to the news release, but instead of spelling out the story, you are seeking to tantalize the reporter or editor. For a pitch to work, the journalists must read your pitch but will put their own stamp on the story, thereby becoming invested in the idea and even getting excited about it. The pitch should contain the subject of this story idea captured in a sentence or phrase, the name of the person to be interviewed along with his or her credentials, and contact information should the journalist wish to follow up.

Here are excerpts from a pitch sent out from Moffitt Cancer Center to a local news program:

"Breast cancer is often linked to women over 50. But young women in their 20s, prime childbearing age, are vulnerable to breast cancer, too. Dr. Pamela Munster knows how damaging breast cancer can be to young women who want to conceive. She offers them hope through a drug she is testing...

"Dr. Munster's clinical trial of 25 women ages 21-25, sponsored by the National Cancer Institute, just went national, so hundreds of women across the country are being treated with this experimental drug.

"Dr. Munster is articulate and can speak in laymen's language. Her presence on your show would also help promote Key to the Cure, next week's four-day shopping event at Saks Fifth Avenue, during which Saks donates 2 percent of sales to Moffitt's women's cancer research...

"Besides breast cancer treatment in young women, Dr. Munster can also discuss the history of hormone

replacement therapy in older women and the recent study by the World Health Organization on breast-cancer risks of HRT."

Keep an eye on the popular culture to determine what's hot and what's not. The popularity of American Idol has sold many a pitch—including a client of PR/PR who ended up in *USA Today*. The newspaper quoted Paul Kowal, president of a telemanagement consulting firm, in a story exploring the fairness of the Idol call-in voting system.

Letter to the editor. The most challenging part of writing a letter is keeping it short. (Put yourself in the editor's shoes: The dreariest part of a letters editor's job is whacking down some thousand-word essay into a publishable few sentences.) Some newspapers will reject letters out of hand if they come in too long. Consult the newspaper's Web site; many will offer a special form that makes submitting your letter easy. A strong, caustic letter often will be chosen for publication over a mild one.

Your letter should make a point. Read the letters in *USA Today* or *The New York Times* for inspiration. Include name, address and contact information. Many newspapers are bedeviled by "fake" letters and letters to which someone else's name has been signed, so they may try to contact you to verify that your letter is for real.

Op-ed piece. Writing an opinion piece will put you or your company on the most prestigious real estate in the newspaper. Many people will read the letters to the editor; far fewer will read the op-ed submission. But those who *do* read will be the political leaders in your community, the activists and others who are likely to influence the opinions of those around them.

An op-ed piece often stakes out ideological territory. In 750 words, it states a case or argues a point of view. As with the media advisory defined above, editors will find your submission almost irresistible if it ties in with a news event.

Tying in with the opening of the Florida Legislature, we sent an op-ed piece out written by Dr. Thomas Brandon, who directs the Tobacco Research and Intervention Program at Moffitt and the University of South Florida. He criticized state policymakers for failing to devote tobacco-tax revenues to tobacco-control programs. Not only did the newspaper in Florida's capital run his piece, but also a second daily newspaper used his writing in an editorial on the subject. The editorial quoted Dr. Brandon:

"It is time for Florida to begin allocating settlement money for tobacco cessation. Funds could be productively used by assisting in the cost of smoking-cessation medications, by promoting and funding clinics to help smokers quit, by funding a first-rate statewide telephone quit line to provide counseling and referrals, by restoring the successful TRUTH campaign aimed at preventing teen smoking."

Note how Dr. Brandon came up with concrete steps the Legislature could take.

That op-ed piece and subsequent editorial helped brand scientists at Moffitt Cancer Center as authorities who not only know their stuff but also are willing to lay it on the line to help their communities. It would have cost the institution $1,693.65 to have bought that much space in the paper.

Letter seeking a correction. At the top of this letter, put "not for publication" in big, bold type. Then outline the mistake that was published or broadcast. Be straightforward and to the point. Avoid blame. (If the reporter has behaved dishonorably or irresponsibly, take this up with the editors by phone.) Request the desired action by requesting either that a written or broadcast correction be made or simply a note attached to the story in the archives so the mistake will not be picked up and disseminated by journalists in the future.

The trade publication article. These are often the easiest to "sell" because the many publications catering to specific industries are always on the lookout for material. A quick e-mail or phone call to the editor can result in immediate acceptance of your 800- to 1,000-word article. Most pieces can follow a simple formula. Start with an anecdote, then summarize the expertise you're about to share. Include a how-to or other checklist of information immediately applicable to the reader.

Checklist for writing for the news media

- use simple declarative sentences

- employ active-voice constructions over the passive voice, which is vague and can seem evasive

- do not indulge in jargon, gobbledygook or bureaucratese

- strive for clarity

- start your news release with the most compelling point and your op-ed piece with the most vital conclusion

- your op-ed piece should conclude on a strong note that echoes the lead paragraph

- quotations should be lively and in plain English, the way people talk in real life

- get the grammar right; doublecheck for consistency in the verb tenses

- rewrite at least once after the first draft is written, breaking up any awkward, convoluted sentences

- make clear in a sentence or phrase why readers or viewers should care about this subject

- vary your sentence length to keep writing from becoming monotonous

- strong nouns that create pictures and verbs that depict action should carry your prose

- remember that adverbs and adjectives generally weaken prose

- use short, plain Saxon words over fancy, obscure Romance words

- remember that you are not writing to express yourself, you are writing to make the reader understand

CHAPTER FOUR

THE NEWS RELEASE: CASE STUDIES, MISSED FIRST STARTS AND EXAMPLES

CHAPTER 4:
The News Release: Case studies, missed first starts and examples

The news release is the staple of the PR industry, for good reason. It is a traditionally brief form of communicating to journalists who you are, what you are about, and why their readers and viewers should care. Crafting a news release is important to launch any newsworthy venture because the information in the news release will form the basis for all your other writing on the subject, including the story pitch and the op-ed piece. You can plan to e-mail and fax news releases throughout the year to publicize events you are planning, to communicate news within your business or to alert journalists that you are available to be interviewed on issues currently in the news.

The reality is that no matter how good *you* think your press release is, most times the release sent out by a novice is doomed even before it is sent. Here are six reasons press releases fail, along with some easy tips to make your release stand out in a crowd.

1. **Bad headline?** Kiss it goodbye. For a variety of reasons, many news releases go straight from the e-mail inbox into the recycle bin. The biggest one is that the headline isn't catchy enough. Writers and editors receive hundreds of releases every day, and most of the time they decide whether or not to read a release based on the headline or subject line. Make sure your release is timely and newsworthy. Finding a relevant story in the newspaper or using

an event guide such as *Chase's Calendar of Events* will give you the edge when it comes to being noticed.

2. **Presenting an irrelevant topic for the audience.** An exciting topic to you might not be as exciting for an editor or writer. Remember, these people are not writing an article to entertain or educate themselves. Their goal is to pass along timely and relevant information to their readers, listeners and viewers. In the end, results are measured on how many magazines or papers are sold or how many people tune it. Whether we like to admit it, these writers are all trying to do the same thing: make money for their respective publications. Don't waste their time with ideas that don't relate to their specific topic.

3. **Including too much self-promotion.** In the example at the end of this chapter, speaker Tara Coyt makes a point to tout her successes and credentials when writing her release, thinking that this will "wow" the editors. In reality, credentials are worthless if your pitch idea lacks merit or your news release is flat. If you provide a good idea backed with solid information, your credentials will speak for themselves. Remember, if you want nothing more than to promote yourself, buy an ad in the publication. The media-savvy individual knows that a good interview doubles as an endorsement and a promotion for themselves and their company.

4. **Dropping the carrot instead of dangling it.** Once you have your release in the hands of a writer or editor and they are interested in your topic, it's time to get to the point and make sure they know what you can talk about.

This is best illustrated in four or five short, concise bullet points along with no more than three examples. While the writers do want to hear what you can offer, they don't want to be bored with a long drawn-out explanation.

5. **Being just another face in the crowd.** The last thing these writers want to see is the same old ideas that any Average Joe can speak on. Make sure you have a creative angle to present to the journalists. Whether or not your ideas are brand new or building on previous research and studies, it is imperative to make them your own. A good exercise for adding individuality to an idea is to sit down and write out 20 different potential hooks. Then walk away from them for an hour or so, come back and decide on the best three. These three will be the basis for why your ideas are different, unique and, more important, meaningful for the writer.

6. **You forgot the "call to action."** Now that you have enchanted editors and writers with your topic, the most important step of the process can take place. Finish your release with a call to action. Make yourself available to the publications for an interview, follow up questions or any other information that they might need. Make sure to include your home phone number, cell phone number and e-mail address at the end of the release. The more contact information they have the better—once they decide to do a story, deadlines click in, and the writer may be in a hurry.

The press release is a useful, important tool in the world of publicity, but it can also be a waste of time if not done properly. With a little extra time and a well-planned idea, you can craft a press release that will give you the best chance of being noticed by writers and editors. Avoid the pitfalls and you could see yourself getting ink in publications in no time.

Make sure to keep an eye on the targeted publications after you send out a news release, or an interview takes place, or an editor agrees to do an article. Many publications will run a piece and will forget to let you know. You could be published and not even know it, so make it a habit to use Internet searches to check for any publications that you might be in.

Trick of the trade: Your grammar and language choices in the news release must be impeccable. Spelling and grammar errors will signal to the editors and writers that you are either poorly educated or that you have not bothered to have your news release proofread. Either circumstance will cause them to doubt your veracity as a source of information. Make grammar and punctuation fun: *The Deluxe Transitive Vampire—a Handbook of Grammar for the Innocent, the Eager and the Doomed* by Karen Elizabeth Gordon is a wonderful reference to have on hand. Other essentials: *The Elements of Style* by William Strunk and E.B. White and *The Associated Press Stylebook* and *Briefing on Media Law*, the most common grammar and style reference in American newsrooms.

A great idea, but a missed first start: What follows is the first draft of a news release. The idea is original. The release *looks* good; the formatting is fine. Try to identify the problems with this draft of the release in your first reading.

College Students use iPods to 'Get Political'

March 2007 (Atlanta) -- College students are using iPods, Icons & Politics to participate in politics and social change with the help of award-winning entrepreneur, Tara Y. Coyt. During a recent college conference in Atlanta, Coyt showed students from Georgia, Illinois, Connecticut and West Virginia how to use iPods and other technology to affect political and social change.

Instead of preaching that students have a 'duty' to get involved Coyt reels them in with technology, popular culture and even beer. "We've got to reach young adults on their turf if we want to win them over. So instead of trying to make them feel guilty, I address their interests and concerns like iPods, entertainers, education and drinking laws."

By the end of her session, held at the national Association for the Promotion of Campus Activities (APCA) conference, African American, Hispanic and white students were discussing specific issues they wanted to resolve and devising tactics to disseminate information to their peers.

Coyt uses her marketing background and tell-it-like-it-is style to convince students that "everyone has an issue" that can be resolved with the use of:

- wide-spread technology (iPods, cell phones and the Internet)
- popular icons (celebrities and symbols)
- politics (students were surprised to learn that they could hold elected positions at age 18)

The response was overwhelming. Natalie Moppert, a student at Greensboro College declared, "I enjoyed your enthusiasm and how you connected the relevance of our age to the

45

importance of politics." Iviana Martinez of Southern Connecticut State University said Coyt "taught me a lot that I can bring to my programming board. Her ideas were very creative and motivating." The students also thanked her for speaking to them on their level and several students even requested that she visit their campus to share the presentation with fellow classmates. In the coming months, Coyt hopes to spread her message on college campuses across the country.

Coyt's history as a student leader and community volunteer enable her to relate to students. She was actively involved in student government, the student newspaper and the Black Student Association while an undergraduate student at Xavier University (Ohio). After graduation Coyt participated in local political campaigns in her hometown of Cleveland, Ohio, became a founding member of The Institute for African American Studies and a Community Forum Leader for the Public Square in Chicago, Illinois.

Recently, during Black History Month Coyt addressed students at Bainbridge College in Bainbridge, GA and has delivered marketing and book development workshops, seminars and training sessions for Kennesaw State University, the Georgia Department of Education, BellSouth, Cingular, Georgia Pacific, Miller, and the Village Writers Group.

Tara Y. Coyt is a member of the Atlanta Technical College Foundation Board, a United Way of Metropolitan Atlanta VIP and a Walter Kaitz Fellow.

Contact information
Tara Y. Coyt
Contact@TaraYCoyt.com
404.441.0883

What's wrong with that first draft? The main problem is that Coyt, who wishes to generate media coverage that will result in more speaking engagements, does not confine herself to one point. With three undeveloped angles, the news release is confusing. The journalist will not know how to proceed, and when that happens, the release goes into cyber oblivion.

Specifically, the three ideas in Coyt's first draft are:

- Coyt gave a talk
- students liked the talk
- the content of the talk was iPods and politics

Whew! That's a lot of ground to cover in a single release.

If the main idea is that Coyt GAVE A TALK, she should stick to that, list credentials, include a testimonial—not a quote from herself as she has done here—and conclude that she is available for interviews on this subject. Then the news release becomes a media advisory, signaling to the journalist that Coyt would like to be contacted by the newspaper or TV station's reporters.

If the main idea is that people LIKED THE TALK, then the release should reflect how Tara Coyt is building momentum with this idea of political activism, once again backed up with appropriate quotes from others as the news release goes along. Facts and figures would shore up this theme as well.

If the main idea is the CONTENT, then Coyt should be more specific. She should move the second paragraph's ideas up to the lead and show HOW she taught them and, equally important, how they intend the use the material.

From the typical editor's standpoint, what is the news value? The news value is not that Coyt gave the talk, or that the students liked it or even what the content of the talk was. The news value is how many college kids she converted and whether the total constitutes a trend. Thus a winning news release would contain some quote from a college kid or kids on how they were going to use this technology in the future. Imagine a "move over, AARP!" slant. AARP has always known the power of numbers and communication. Wouldn't they sweat buckets over the idea of college kids becoming a voting bloc? A quote from an AARP spokesperson could add the conflict that every news story needs.

Too, a backup proofreader or editor might have caught errors such as "affect change" (it should be "effect change") and help weed out clichés such as, "The response was over-whelming." Other problems: The headline verb "use" is weak. "Award-winning" is inappropriate in the first sentence. A news release *must* avoid overheated rhetoric. A news release should be hype-free and meticulously accurate, not self-promotional.

After receiving this feedback, Coyt took another shot at the release. Here is her improved version:

iPods Convert Students to Political Activism

March 2007 (Atlanta) -- It only took an hour for college students to commit themselves to address issues near and dear to them, such as education and health insurance. Students like Aracely Gutierrez of Morton College praised Atlanta business owner, Tara Coyt and her revolutionary program, iPods, Icons & Politics saying, "She made sure we understood exactly what we can do to get our issues/message across."

Before the session ended students huddled in small groups developing a 'plan of attack' utilizing iPods, the Internet and popular culture to reach their peers and elected officials. Iviana Martinez of Southern Connecticut State University said Coyt, "taught me a lot that I can bring to my programming board. Her ideas were very creative and motivating."

The workshop, held at the national Association for the Promotion of Campus Activities (APCA) conference successfully sparked political involvement in college students and gave them practical tools to disseminate information. Kyle Huie of Greensboro College said, "The session was very informative and really talked about good ways to get people involved." Natalie Moppert another Greensboro student declared, "I enjoyed how you connected the relevance of our age to the importance of politics."

The students called on Coyt to share the presentation with fellow classmates and thanked her for speaking to them on their level. Jessica Hamilton of Brazesport College, who plans to become a political journalist proclaimed, "You really helped me understand how to persuade, shape and affect a readers thinking."

The success of iPods, Icons & Politics lies in the ability to reach students "where they are," presenting them with success stories and making it easy to get involved by using technology, entertainment and popular culture. Coyt was thrilled to witness the transformation as students moved from reservation and apathy to activism. In the coming months, she plans to spread her message on college campuses across the country.

As a student at Xavier University (Ohio) Tara Coyt was actively involved in student government, the student newspaper and the Black Student Association. After graduation she participated in local political campaigns in her hometown of

Cleveland, Ohio, became a founding member of The Institute for African American Studies and a Community Forum Leader for the Public Square in Chicago, Illinois.

Coyt is a member of the Atlanta Technical College Foundation Board, a United Way of Metropolitan Atlanta VIP and a Walter Kaitz Fellow. Recently, during Black History Month she addressed students at Bainbridge College in Bainbridge, GA and has delivered marketing and book development workshops, seminars and training sessions for Kennesaw State University, the Georgia Department of Education, BellSouth, Cingular, Georgia Pacific, Miller, and the Village Writers Group.

Tara Y. Coyt
Coyt Communications
www.CoytCommunications.com
404.441.0883

Clearly, this second draft is meatier. However, it still sounds less like a news release and more like a piece of self-promotional marketing literature. Let's see if we can isolate and accent the news value so that a journalist's interest might be piqued. Remember, the goal of a news release is either to have it printed verbatim or to inspire a journalist to write his or her own story on the topic. Let's make the news release shorter yet more enticing:

NEWS RELEASE

ATTENTION: news editors, political reporters, lifestyle editors
NOTE: Georgia, Illinois, Connecticut and West Virginia mentioned

iPods Not Just for Entertainment Anymore: Can You Spell Revolution-in-the-Making? (Move Over, AARP!)

March 2007 (Atlanta) -- And you thought those college students with their ears glued to iPods were just listening to music! Not so—a gathering of students at the recent Association for the Promotion of Campus Activities national conference learned that the ubiquitous entertainment device can help them rule the world, or at least effect drastic political change.

"We've got to reach young adults on their turf if we want to win them over and motivate them to become active participants in democracy," says Tara Y. Coyt, a student leader in her college days who now delivers marketing and book-development workshops, seminars and training sessions. "So instead of trying to make them feel guilty, I address their interests such as iPods and entertainers and their concerns such as education and drinking laws."

After only an hour, the college students committed themselves to try to prod politicians and their own peers on issues such as health insurance. Aracely Gutierrez of Morton College said, "She made sure we understood exactly what we can do to get our messages across."

Before the session ended, students from Georgia, Illinois, Connecticut and West Virginia huddled in small groups developing a "plan of attack," identifying issues to resolve and devising creative ways to employ iPods, the Internet and even icons of popular culture when waging a campaign of ideas.

Many of the students were amazed to find out they could hold elected positions at the age of 18. Natalie Moppert, a student at Greensboro College, said Coyt "connected the relevance of our age to the importance of politics."

In the coming months, Coyt hopes to spread her message on college campuses across the country.

About Tara Y. Coyt: Tara Y. Coyt of Coyt Communications (www.CoytCommunications.com) is a Walter Kaitz Fellow and a member of the Atlanta Technical College Foundation Board. Her workshop clients include the Georgia Department of Education, Kennesaw State University, BellSouth, Cingular and Georgia Pacific.

For more information please call 404.441.0883 or e-mail Tara@CoytCommunications.com

This news release version, in fewer words, gives editors and reporters all the information they need to follow up. Note choice of facts, quotes and wording. This news release carries its own little story, enticing the journalist to either publish the news release or pick up the phone to find out more.

Checklist for news releases

- Have at least two careful proofreaders read behind you

- Present your topic in an enthusiastic, effective manner

- Briefly define your credentials and achievements as they relate to the topic

- Size matters: try to keep the release to one page

- Include documentation to back up any assertions

- Include attribution of all facts and figures

- "Localize" the release by including references to people and things in the community

- Remember that your goal is to motivate the media to seek you out for more information

CHAPTER FIVE

THE 15 MOST COMMON PUBLICITY MISTAKES PEOPLE MAKE

CHAPTER 5:

The 15 Most Common
Publicity Mistakes People Make

As a business owner, you probably know that publicity is important to your success. But many entrepreneurs, speakers and authors (and maybe you're one of them) make crucial mistakes in their publicity campaigns. While some of the mistakes are more detrimental than others, the actual costs can be staggering.

For example, saying the wrong thing to a reporter may only cost you a quote in a national magazine. But in terms of advertising dollars, that quote could have been worth hundreds. And you never really know who might have read the interview. Maybe a reporter for *USA Today*? Maybe Oprah's producer (or maybe even Oprah herself)? Plus, what about all the time, money and effort you spent in getting that reporter on the phone?

It's true; everyone makes mistakes. By being aware of the more common ones, at least you can take action to avoid them. If you want to make the most of every publicity opportunity that comes your way, avoid the following mistakes that novices commonly make in their publicity campaigns:

1. **Thinking hundreds of customers will walk through their door from one hit.** Fame and name recognition take time and repetition to build. In fact, a person will need to see your name and logo about six or seven times before

they actually remember it. So regardless of what you've heard, there's no such thing as an overnight success.

2. **Not being unique in their approach.** No one wants to hear the same old message over and over again. So develop a hook—a unique angle that sets your business apart from others. For example, if you own a restaurant, consider what's unique about it. What's unique about your menu? Has the restaurant been family-owned and operated for generations? Do you offer vegetarian cuisine? The more you can make your message unique or different from the "old way," the more attention you'll attract.

3. **Thinking they can't get into a large publication.** Many small business owners, speakers and authors feel intimidated by the big-name publications. They envision high-powered magazine editors schmoozing with Fortune 500 CEOs and lining up interviews with well-known figureheads for the next six months. In reality, editors scramble daily to find people to interview who have knowledge on the latest trends and topics. Realize, too, that editors must find new, fresh and exciting people to interview either weekly or monthly, so the more knowledgeable people they can add to their databases, the better. Make yourself stand out as a reliable information source and you will get the media's attention. Here are some examples from the PR/PR client files: *Reader's Digest* mentioned paperwork organizer and productivity expert Barbara Hemphill. *The New York Times*, ABC News and *USA Today* quoted Dr. Maurice Ramirez of the American Board of Disaster Medicine. *Working Women* and other national magazines

published an article by business consultant Don Andersson, and the *Los Angeles Times* interviewed him.

4. **Thinking small publications don't matter.** Even big name businesses had to build their expertise and name recognition by starting out with mentions in small publications and trade journals. Although such publications aren't sold on newsstands, you never know who's reading them. Pam Ammondson, for instance, started out with an interview in *Escape* magazine. Who's ever heard of that publication? Turns out a writer for *Time* magazine read the piece, in fact. He soon called Ammondson for a *Time* story. Next thing she knew, Tom Brokaw was on the line—literally. Ammondson ended up on NBC News with her ideas about employee sabbaticals and burnout. So don't overlook small publications as a foundation for your publicity efforts.

5. **Thinking their ideas are wonderful.** Touting your experience and explaining all the reasons why your business is wonderful to an editor is not an effective way to pitch your ideas. In fact, this is an immediate turn-off. Realize that an editor or reporter cares only about one thing: their readers or viewers. Instead of telling the editors all about your ideas and your business, first learn about their readers and what they want. If you can identify one of their readers' or viewers' problems and position yourself as an expert with ideas to solve it, you're well on your way to a successful story pitch.

6. **Pitching themselves instead of a story idea.** For the moment, forget about your great resume and experience. First, pitch a publication or program's editors and producers

by highlighting the benefits you or your business can offer their readers or viewers. Consider what uniqueness you can offer and why their readers or viewers will find what you have to say compelling.

7. **Pitching the wrong person.** Besides wasting your time and theirs, pitching your ideas to the wrong media person will likely frustrate them. If you have an article you'd like to publish, you need to talk to an editor. But if you want to score an interview, you need a reporter's interest. If you have written a book about, say, the business of sports, you might want to talk to the book-review editor or to a sports reporter. If you call the news desk, prepare to be treated brusquely.

8. **Not finding out what reporters, producers and editors really want.** As you present your idea to reporters, producers and editors ask questions about what they're looking for and what their audience is looking for. Then make changes to your initial idea based on their responses. Don't try to "sell" your idea if it isn't a good fit; instead, promote alternate ideas and emphasize your ability to address a variety of issues. That way if your story pitch doesn't fly, you'll at least end up in the database—and perhaps quoted in a different story down the road.

9. **Not answering the reporter's questions.** Always let the reporter or interviewer lead the conversation, because they most likely have an agenda for the story's development already in mind. Don't attempt to take over the conversation or talk about points the reporter doesn't want to cover. They simply won't include you in the final story. Feel free to create context. But first be aware of the reporter's angle.

10. **Not getting to the point.** Audiences and readers love to hear firsthand accounts of experiences relating to the topic because it helps them know you on a more personal level. But don't overload the reporter with unnecessary information that isn't directly related to the story, and don't ramble. If you can't convey your message in a short amount of time, then your answer (whether quote or soundbite) won't be used.

11. **Not respecting the reporter's time.** Reporters work through repeated deadlines with a great sense of urgency, and nothing will irritate them more than you being inconsiderate. So before you start pitching your ideas, always ask if they are on deadline. If yes, ask for a more convenient callback time. Sometimes you can say, "Oh, I was just going to leave a quick voicemail about a story idea; I didn't expect you to answer, and I'm about to run." This statement can relax the reporter, because he or she knows you are not in a position to monopolize their time—you're busy, too!

12. **Not gearing their pitches to the specific publication.** If you get a "no" response from an editor, reporter or producer, always ask, "What don't you like?" Then adapt your presentation on the spot. The more you learn about their needs and customize your message for their specific audience, the more likely you'll be featured in their publication or on their show. Case in point: PR/PR client Pam Ammondson. She wrote an article touting six-month sabbaticals as a way for professionals to refresh themselves mid-career. Many executive-oriented magazines hated the idea, understandably loath to promote the concept of their top talent disappearing for half the year. After dozens

of turndowns, Ammondson retooled the piece with the theme "prevent employee burnout," and several national publications snapped up the article.

13. **Making their pitch an advertisement for their products or services.** Authors spend a large portion of their time selling their books because the profession simply demands it. But interviews and articles are not the right places to go on and on about your expertise and knowledge. You must let your information speak for itself. By giving solid, useable information, audiences will automatically know how great your book is. The same principle holds for other businesses.

14. **Not providing their publicist with material and information in a timely manner.** Business owners are busy—that's a given. But so are publicists, editors and reporters. For your information to get into the right people's hands, you need to give your publicist the requested information ASAP. Your publicist can't pitch you, your ideas, your company or your book unless he or she has the most relevant information about you that showcases all you have to offer in a positive way. And if you make your publicist wait for information to send an editor or reporter, you may miss your chance to get interviewed or featured in your desired media outlet.

15. **Not understanding the importance of frequency of publicity.** While it takes a long time to build your name recognition in the marketplace, it takes no time at all for people to forget about you. So you have to maintain the frequency of your publicity throughout the life of your business, especially when your competition maintains the frequency of theirs. Otherwise, you become old news.

Trick of the trade: Many if not most reporters and editors dread phone calls, especially those from people who fail to understand their harried schedules. Find out how the reporter prefers to be contacted. Sources such as the Bacon's directory of newsrooms publish lists. Media-relations consultants within your hometown community have this information as well. Some reporters spell out in their telephone greetings, "if you are from a public-relations company, please use e-mail to communicate." Some reporters and editors prefer to receive story ideas via snail mail or fax. You'll have your best shot at getting what you want if you stick to the journalists' contact preferences.

The rest of this chapter will bolster your knowledge of the news media, helping you avoid embarrassing media mix-ups.

You cannot hope to deal effectively with the news media if you fail to understand the distinction between genres. Newspapers and broadcast entities, along with Web news sites and blogs, are different animals. They report differently, write differently and in some cases think differently.

Newspaper reporters operate on daily deadlines. Television reporters may have a series of deadlines: early morning, noon, evening and late night. Ditto for radio reporters. Web journalists (even the amateurs) have immediate deadlines, 24/7. Cable stations that offer 24-hour news coverage also have constant deadlines.

In addition to the actual moment the pages go to press or the show goes on the air, the reporter must observe internal deadlines so that editors have time to review the stories.

This constant pressure creates impatience as an occupational hazard. You may find that reporters are a class of people who might otherwise be fun, bright and likable were they not constantly and single-mindedly interviewing, researching and writing—all with an editor breathing down their necks.

The Internet has made reporters' jobs both easier and harder. They receive literally hundreds of e-mails a day. Some of those e-mails are from people who are trying to convince them to provide news coverage of their pet product, institution or person. Other communications come from people who are reacting, sometimes negatively, to stories the reporter has written recently. The reporter must deal with all these while pulling together a story for the next day's newspaper.

Whether you are actively pitching stories or simply waiting for the reporter on your beat to contact you, you can benefit from an understanding of newsroom setup. Setup is different from one media organization to the next, but newspaper newsrooms have a great deal in common and so do television newsrooms.

Newspapers. Most newsrooms are set up in an almost military-style hierarchy. The person who wields the most power over what will become the day's lead story depends on the size of the newspaper. It could be the executive editor, managing editor or city editor. In a daily news conference, the relative merits of stories are bruited about, and sometimes consensus drives decisions about news value are made.

Other times, the ranking editor has the last word. The reporter may have little to say about the story's positioning, and the reporter is not the one who writes the headline—he or she may not even see the headline before going home for the day. (Remember this if you ever have cause to complain about a headline. If the headline is inaccurate, the reporter is as likely to be as distressed as you are.)

Another overall distinction you must understand is the difference between news and editorial. The news department and editorial department at credible newspapers are different, independent of each other and devoted to maintaining these distinctions. The editorial board researches, writes and publishes the so-called "opinion of the newspaper" in unsigned editorials. If they have time, editorial writers will contact you directly to verify that information in the news story is correct. Often they don't have time, so outreach on your part can be vital.

Editorial writers are deemed more influential within the newsroom hierarchy because, while reporters are duty-bound to be fair, editorial writers can use the pen to praise or punish. A well-reasoned or passionate editorial in a popular newspaper can make or break an institution, organization or agency.

Here are some of the common jobs in the newsroom.

The *managing editor* runs the show. Depending on the size of the newspaper, he or she may be intimately involved as reporters ferret out the day's news. The managing editor is often caught up in supervisory activities.

The *city editor* or *metro editor* often orchestrates coverage of the local city or cities, county and perhaps even state. He or she makes assignments, determines priorities and juggles the whereabouts of reporters.

Reporters cover a defined area, such as education, health or City Hall. At smaller papers, reporters are expected to stay on top of multiple areas, which usually means many stories go unreported.

The *features editor* oversees stories that are less hard-hitting and more likely to appeal to interests such as lifestyle, social trends and personalities.

Over in the editorial department, the *editorial page editor* decides which topics will merit an editorial and who will write them. He or she will also decide which of the competing visitors who want to pay a visit (and press a cause) will be granted an audience. Most editorial boards endorse political candidates at election time. The editorial page editor is answerable to the publisher.

Editorial writers are members of the editorial board, which as a group may decide editorial policy on certain subjects, take field trips and interview political candidates to make a determination on whom to endorse. They often have beats, just like reporters, but they are not expected to respond to every daily occurrence. They are likely to weigh in with an opinion only when an editorial may be influential in the situation.

The newspaper's *publisher* may have come up through the ranks of the business side of the newspaper (either circulation or advertising). He or she may be appalled when the news or editorial departments print unflattering stories about business or civic leaders. However, good publishers keep their noses out of the newsrooms so that the newspaper can maintain integrity and a reputation for independence.

While daily newspapers in America are suffering drastic declines, they still reach a majority of the population segments deemed "influential" by marketers and policymakers.

Television. TV reporters must think visual, visual, visual. They need pictures of what they are talking about. They prefer B-roll, or original shots of people or things to show while they are explaining the story. They will settle for still photos or graphics if that's all that is available.

TV reporters are also bound by the genre in other ways. Highly complex stories involving multiple sources or institutions, abstract concepts and hard-to-explain motivations probably will not fly on TV. The story *must* be reducible to a one-sentence tease.

Most TV news personnel are very poorly paid except for the anchors. You might be shocked to learn the salary of the reporter who is interviewing you. Especially in small communities, their wages can hit below federal poverty guidelines. They are doing the work because they are ambitious and hope to move to larger markets or simply because they love it.

Just as in newspapers, *reporters* frequently cover a beat. However, newsroom staffs are much smaller at TV stations compared with newspapers, so reporters constantly face being pulled into general-assignment work. However, many reporters specialize in a particular area—say, health care—so you may talk to the same person repeatedly and thus establish a relationship.

Unlike reporters, who can stay on a beat for many years and become veterans, the people running the newsroom are likely to be in their 20s and 30s. The hours are long, the pace is urgent and the pay is low. For some roles in the TV newsroom, there are different people for the morning and afternoon slots.

Producers go along with reporters on shoots if possible and decide story angle and visuals. They are active in staging soundbites and B-roll. Back at the station, they either edit the piece or determine the direction of the editing. A TV station in a large market will have separate *field producers* who accompany reporters and are distinct from producers in the studio, who determine the content of a story, newscast or show.

The *assignment editor* deploys reporters on the stories of the day. A key decision maker, this person can pull a reporter off one story and on to another if a more compelling breaking news event has occurred.

The *anchor* may or may not be actively involved in reporting some stories. Most anchors are not merely newsreaders. They help make decisions about story play. Like editorial writers at newspapers, they gravitate toward stories that interest them. It is good to have an anchor who is interested in a topic you care about because you are more likely to gain coverage. The downside is that the anchor has limited time to put together a story.

Radio. Considerations for TV news mostly apply to radio as well. One difference is that many radio stations are much smaller in terms of staff. Radio reporters are not concerned at all with visuals, but they are very likely to be highly concerned with sound quality. They sometimes exhibit a better grasp of the story they are reporting, because they require a thorough grounding in the facts so that they can paint a word picture for the listener. Many radio programs have daily shows with an almost insatiable appetite for new guests.

Internet. Don't make the mistake of discounting the Internet. Millions of news sites exist worldwide from one year to the next. A story that originates locally can make it across the globe with the click of a mouse. Some of these news sites are highly credible. What's more, the blog has created a whole new class of journalists. Depending on how provocative, gutsy or amusing the individual is, or how compelling his or her subject matter is, a blogger can command a huge following. Corporations are going to school on how to deal with bloggers who criticize them.

A podcast can acquaint millions of people around the world with your name and image overnight.

While it is true that much of the information posted on the Web cannot be verified, consumers by the millions are turning to this resource. Where else can you research a topic and be rewarded with news, encyclopedia entries, video clips, message boards, links to organizations and live chats with experts? With what other medium can you connect directly with the public?

Within the media outlined above are a number of vehicles for getting your story out. When conversing with a journalist, always remember that he or she has nothing to do with advertisements, which are paid for by the advertiser. (In the PR and political consulting trade, news coverage is sometimes referred to as "free media.")

Within the newspaper, you can pay for an *advertisement*. You can convince a reporter to write a *news story* or an editorial writer to write an *editorial*. You can write a *letter to the editor*, which is a good idea when you seek visibility because the letters page is well read. An *op-ed column* is also a possibility, especially if you are an expert in a certain field. These run on the opinion pages, usually opposite the editorial page, and should be kept to about 700 words. (More about this in later chapters.)

Television news similarly offers different vehicles of coverage, including the paid *advertisement*. There is also the possibility of creating a *Public Service Announcement* and persuading the station to run it. As with newspapers, you may be the subject of a *news story*. Many stations also offer *public-affairs programs*, where your organization can provide a specialist to sit on a panel of "talking heads." In larger markets, TV stations have *magazine programs*, which are fluffier than the news show, seek to reflect the community and are always on the lookout for human-interest content.

The distinctions among media may seem impossibly complex. They are simple. A rudimentary refresher before you deal with journalists is all you need to understand where they are coming from and what they seek.

Checklist for avoiding journalists' pet peeves.

Don't:

- contact reporters with a story idea that is outside of their beat or unsuitable for their medium

- work from old media lists when sending e-mail or snail mail; staff changes and turnover are common in the media

- promise you will deliver an interview, the names of sources and contacts or a written piece and then fail to come through

- write news releases in which the most important information is buried

- repeatedly call reporters to see if they are going to follow up on your news release

Do:

- know the difference between a news story, feature article, column, letter to the editor and other forms of coverage

- familiarize yourself with your local media's news cycles and deadlines

- establish that you are willing to answer reporters' questions, even if that means a little digging on your part for the accurate information

- cooperate as the reporter navigates his or her way through your organization and enlist the cooperation of others

- tell the news media about an event you know they will want to cover well in advance so they can make plans

CHAPTER
SIX

SCORING POSITIVE PUBLICITY—PART I: 7
WAYS TO PREPARE, 7 TACTICS TO TRY

CHAPTER 6:

Scoring Positive Publicity—Part I:
7 ways to prepare, 7 tactics to try

Now that you understand the nature of news, you may be asking yourself: "How can I generate news when I don't see any conflict?!" Not to worry. First, there may be conflict that you have not yet recognized as such. Second, not all conflict is bad, negative or controversial.

Besides, while conflict guarantees a high placement in the day's order of the news, editors know that the public cannot take a steady drumbeat of dour happenings. They will always make place in the news lineup for a bright human-interest story. What's more, many media outlets, influenced by the "public journalism" movement, believe it is part of their duty to accurately reflect their communities. And not *everything* in their communities is going wrong. *The Tampa Tribune*, for instance, recently devoted the majority of its Sunday opinion section to personality profiles of its regular letter writers in the community.

Unless you are a rapper whose music sales go up when the publicity gets raunchy, you and your organization or business probably want to be a story of what's going right.

Publicity will help you create and cement a good reputation, which will help you achieve top-of-mind recognition with your clients and, if you operate a nonprofit, support from your state politicians. Notice how well-known businesses don't advertise just once. Car dealers, furniture outlets and banks advertise constantly, knowing that it may be months or even years before you need their services. But when you do, their business names will be firmly embedded in your mind.

The same principle applies to "free media" coverage. If you are an unknown or new business, and you are seeking clients, you need to get your name into the public arena so that customers will gravitate to you. If you are a public speaker, media coverage will give you a patina of glam that will set you apart from other speakers. If you are a large nonprofit, or even a small one, chances are good that you must rely on the good will of the legislature in your state or on donors in your community. A consistently rosy image in the news media will help create those positive public perceptions needed to keep your financial foundation firm.

People need to see things at least seven times to even remember it. When someone reads about you in an article, they may not have a need for your services or products at that particular moment. But by continually having your name out there, they will begin to recognize it, and when the time comes they will remember seeing your name.

One story on one day is a good thing. But you'll need more than that to generate interest and create an image that will shore you up during bad or indifferent times. Consistent mentions of your organization over time are needed to create awareness among a public deluged with commercial and other messages.

Trick of the trade: Get your name out everywhere. Don't, say, dismiss a magazine as being too small. If the editors want an article or interview from you, do it. Many times a larger magazine or newspaper will pick up stories from smaller publications. You could have originally interviewed for a small local paper and have the *Wall Street Journal*

---

or *USA Today* pick the story up. Similarly, don't discount a publication because you don't think it fits your target audience. You never know who is reading what. Maybe one person will have read an article you are quoted in and then passed it along to a friend in another industry who has a need for your product or service. A little article in *Laundry Today*, an industry newsletter, prompted an industry trade association to reward the author with a lucrative speaking engagement. Sy Sperling, founder of the Hair Club for Men, became a client of PR/PR when he read a trade-publication article Pam Lontos wrote for a multilevel marketing magazine—a friend had sent it to him, thinking he'd be interested!

Here are seven steps to take as you prepare to reach out to the news media.

1. **Teach yourself to recognize a good-news story.** Look for them within your organization or your life. Have recent hirings occurred on a scale that would interest the local business reporter? Are there any sweet human coincidences? Did two people from across the globe—say, Chernobyl—meet at your workplace and marry? True, the story will be about them, not you. But your business or institution's name will be mentioned. If you are the immigration lawyer who helped them get into America, your name will have a place in the story. One mention of your name—that's a good goal for one day's news cycle.

2. **Realistically assess the news value of the story.** To do otherwise is to brand yourself an amateur with the news media. Plus you will create unrealistic expectations at your workplace and set yourself up for disappointment. You may be excited about a particular occurrence or event. However, if you are close to the event, you may have lost perspective. What you think is newsworthy may in fact be something that is happening routinely throughout the community or the nation, diminishing its news value.

When a local bank gave a million-dollar donation to the H. Lee Moffitt Cancer Center & Research Institute, for instance, staff members of the Moffitt Foundation were incredulous and downcast when the daily newspapers in Tampa and St. Petersburg ignored the story. They couldn't understand why news reporters had failed to throng to the news conference. In addition to the news conference being held at exactly the wrong time (5 p.m., hitting *everyone's* tightest deadline), the elements of the story predictably were too weak to get on news writers' radar screens.

As one reporter explained only half cynically, "If Senator Connie Mack, Moffitt's chairman of the board, were the source of the million dollars, and he funneled it through the bank because they are blackmailing him by threatening to expose some illegal shenanigans, then we'll cover it." Was she being mean or sarcastic? Not really. She simply overstated her lack of interest because too many public-relations representatives had been pestering her lately, seeking to convince her to turn business-as-usual into news. The fact of the matter is that, beyond a brief mention in the business-news section, neither of the two major metropolitan daily newspapers considered the story to be news. Million-dollar donations to charities are expected from big banks, for one thing; for another, reporters believe that big businesses make lavish donations precisely because they are seeking publicity. Therefore, the news conference needed a new angle or an unexpected twist to make it compelling.

Remember that reporters are looking for something of human interest, something new and timely with facts to back it up. It is your job to show them how the story will benefit their readers, viewers or listeners.

3. **Be persistent.** If you have left a message but don't hear back right away, follow up. Sometimes you contact a reporter, share an idea, and he or she wants to complete the interview by 3 p.m. Other times, story placements take months or more. Barbara Hemphill, a client of PR/PR and author of *Taming the Paper Tiger*, once had an excellent story to pitch. It took a month to get the targeted magazine reporter on the phone. After thinking about the proposed story, the reporter passed but suggested an editor at the same publication. The editor spent a couple of months mulling the idea over, then declined but was kind enough to suggest yet a third possible writer, again at the same publication. This whole process took a year, but the results were worth it—a story about Hemphill in a national magazine.

4. **Consider timing because your idea is more valuable when it is the direct opposite of bad news.** If your organization is doing something to, say, help people find jobs, the idea will have more dramatic appeal during a time of high-profile layoffs. Watch the headlines in your industry. If you have invented a new propeller guard, pitch it to the news media right after a weekend in which boaters have killed

manatees—or right before summer when boating season reaches its peak. A routine story about new advances in fish farming will have more jazz at a time when a net ban in coastal areas has put commercial fishermen out of work. A drug company patenting a new treatment for a particular disease can generate more stories when someone famous dies from that disease.

A case in point: At the National Comprehensive Cancer Network's 12th annual conference in Fort Lauderdale in March of 2007, several national news publications covered a panel that debated solutions to the high cost of new anti-cancer drugs. Normally, a panel discussion would be considered a snoozer. But the panel came one day after a news story in which a Wall Street analyst predicted the spectacularly high cost of new anti-cancer drugs would spark a backlash from patients and the public. Because of this wonderful timing, an otherwise dry discussion forum became fodder for a *Business Week* editor's future stories, while United Press International carried a daily piece, and U.S. and European Internet news sites that carry Business Wire picked up a news release within hours of the event.

5. **Before you contact the news media, make sure you have all the facts on hand.** Be ready with what they will need—contact information for the primary source within your organization as well as the names and numbers of other people they might wish to interview. Anticipate questions and know your stuff. How many people within your organization or business worked on this project? How many constituents will it affect? Provide context. If you are a health organization bringing a new treatment method or machine to town, do a LexisNexis search to make sure

other organizations in your state or region haven't beaten you to the punch.

6. **Understand which editor or reporter will be interested.** Don't bore the city editor with a heart-tugging people story that the newspaper usually confines to the feature pages. Don't expect a general-interest reporter to understand the significance of how your company's spinoff may affect the stock market. Don't expect a TV reporter to salivate over a story for which there are no pictures. Make sure you have done your homework before contacting a news organization. You can share your clips to leverage one form of publicity for another. For example, if you are pitching a reporter who covers banking, feel free to fax or e-mail tear sheets of articles you have written for financial trade and association magazines.

7. **Come up with a fun phrase or gimmick.** If you do this brilliantly, your story could quickly go national. Consider how The Center for Consumer Freedom punched holes in the National Institutes of Health's BMI. Remember BMI—Body Mass Index? You don't hear much about it anymore because of the exposure of the flawed premises on which it was based.

When the BMI first came out, millions of people discovered that the federal government classified them as obese even though they didn't look all that big in the mirror. The "epic of obesity" began to hurt the restaurant industry, which decided to fight back.

It turns out the Body Mass Index doesn't take muscle mass into account. Therefore a whole host of celebrities qualified as obese, including President Bush and Governor

Schwarzenegger. The PR company hired to blast the BMI decided on a low-budget approach. They created a Web site where people could plug in their height and weight and see whether the government considered them obese.

Amusing press releases exposed the flawed standard, renaming it the "Bull Malarkey Index." The Consumer Freedom group garnered publicity in the nation's largest newspapers including *The New York Times* and networks including Fox and NBC.

Remember, it's rare that a person will become an overnight success from one hit. Usually that first article or interview is the start of a long road—a building block in the success you are reaching for. To build fame, you need repetition. Your name must be in front of decision makers over and over again before it will sink in. You never know where someone will see your name and decide to give you a call.

Here are seven ways to jumpstart the process of getting your name out there.

1. **News releases.** With some PR practitioners, the news release has fallen out of favor. Conventional thinking is that journalists never use them to generate story ideas. In fact, journalists do scan brief, well-written releases and occasionally use them as a basis for stories. At the H. Lee Moffitt Cancer Center & Research Institute, an ordinary news release prompted the health writer of the *Los Angeles Times* to write about a chemical wafer inserted in the brains of patients during brain-tumor surgery.

There is almost no downside to doing a news release. If reporters are too busy to bother, they will simply throw the news release in the trash with no ill will generated.

Subconsciously, though, the fact will register that you or your organization are "out there" being proactive, even if the news release doesn't spark a story that day.

All but the most complex situations are fairly easy to capture in a one-page news release. Fill it with who-what-when-where-why. Lead off with a hook to make the reporter or editor understand why people should care about the story. Don't force the editor to read between the lines to figure out what is important. Include a quotation from someone in your company. Always include contact information so a reporter or assignment editor can follow up.

Refer again to Chapter 4. Each paragraph should contain no more than three sentences, and each sentence should consist of 30-35 words. Omit hype, jargon and acronyms. Let your story stand on its own merits. If your company is too small to support a media-relations staff, outsourcing is relatively inexpensive. In most markets you can contract to have a simple news release researched and written for from $200 to $400.

2. **Old-fashioned pitching.** Don't beg, plead or grovel unless you know the reporter really well and can have some fun with him or her. But do ask. Reporters and editors sitting in newsrooms and overloaded with beat requirements can't possibly know everything that is going on in their communities. They rely on people to let them know about good stories out there.

As with the news release, keep your story pitch succinct and to the point. Make it obvious why readers and listeners would be interested in this story. Make sure you understand the target audience of the journalist before making a pitch. A reporter who writes only about new technology, say, may be offended if you pitch a story about a health trend, because you have revealed yourself as someone unfamiliar with his or her work.

Unless you have discovered that a particular reporter or editor hates phone calls, you might be able to pitch a story by phone. If the reporter answers, or if you get voicemail, speak in bullet points, but don't sound rehearsed. Have a sheet in front of you containing the key selling points of the story, along with brief background information.

Catching an editor on the phone can be to your advantage, because you should always be prepared to come up with more than one story angle to pitch in case the first one doesn't pan out. For instance, if your story idea flops because the media outlet has just done one that's too similar, don't ring off without making a second try. "Oh, you just assigned a story on the high cost of anti-cancer drugs? How about one on how the Patient Advocate Foundation is connecting poor people with millions in aid offered by the pharmaceutical industry?" If you can think on your feet, you can sometimes offer the very story the editor is looking for at the moment.

3. **Writing letters to the editor.** The dirty little secret of daily newspapers is the popularity of the letters section. Journalists scramble to ferret out facts, dig for the truth, verify, do extensive research and write deathless prose. How do readers reward them? By flipping immediately to the opinion section to read the often-uninformed ideas proffered by others in the community. This fact may appall reporters and editors, but you can use it to your advantage.

Watch the news and see what is making the headlines. When the subject matter overlaps your areas of interest, write a letter. The hard part will be to keep it to 150 or 250 words, but this restriction is crucial. Many newspapers are swamped with letters. They don't want to deal with slogging through a long letter and cutting it to the size required for publication. Your letter will have a better chance of seeing print if you stick to the word limit.

Letters most likely to be chosen for publication are those that stake out territory in the marketplace of ideas and make strong arguments for a particular point of view. Check out the lists of daily newspapers at American Journalism Review's Internet site, *ajr.org*.

4. **Writing op-ed pieces.** Like letters, the op-ed piece should put forth a point of view. As with the news release and a story pitch, the question "why you should care" should be dealt with at the top of the story. Op-ed pieces are often written by experts who do research in a particular area. (More about this in Chapter 7.)

Researchers have a tendency to save their juiciest conclusions for the end of the piece, because that is the structure expected in an article submitted to peer-reviewed journals. The structure of the op-ed piece is the complete opposite. The conclusion or most compelling fact *must* come first. Well-crafted arguments should follow, making a clear case and concluding with a call to action.

Before attempting to write an op-ed piece, read several of them in local and national newspapers to gain a feel for how they are done. You can have a staff member ghost-write for you or your CEO or hire a freelancer.

Your op-ed piece will hit home with editors if you can combine a gutsy, passionate approach with a logical analysis of a situation. As with any other form of writing submitted to the news media, language must be clear, punchy and direct. Editors will read for clarity; they will screen out any piece that lacks appeal to the average reader.

A brief bio-note outlining the author's credentials should be added to the end of the piece to save the opinion editor from the work of tracking that information down. An op-ed piece should be kept to about 700 or 750 words. Editors are often likely to be most receptive to pieces written by someone within the local community.

5. **Staging events.** Grand openings, symposia or town-hall meetings are examples of events that typically draw news coverage. Make sure an experienced event planner is handling or at least supervising the preparations to avoid embarrassment in front of the public and the news media. Give the media plenty of notice. Make sure all of the technical needs of the electronic media are accounted for, such as electrical outlets.

6. **Conducting a poll.** Large polling organizations don't have a lock on polling. You can create a poll, too. Just make sure you know the difference between a scientific, randomized survey and an informal poll and *never* overstate the results. You can draw conclusions from scientific surveys about what people believe within a small margin of error. Informal polls are useful *only* to suggest reactions and create public interest.

Sometimes research companies in your community will be able to conduct a survey at an affordable price. No matter what your business, a survey can no doubt be crafted so that you can ascertain how people feel about an issue you can relate to your company.

Do you think it is coincidence that national advertising campaigns for new pharmaceuticals to aid sleep are launched right after surveys that claim many Americans are sleep deprived?

7. **Writing for the weeklies.** While daily newspapers are on the decline, many weeklies are experiencing new popularity, because people want to know what is going on in their neck of the woods. One thing that hasn't changed is the low-budget nature of the weekly. Staffs are tiny. Many only have one or two reporters or none at all. If you or someone on your staff can write, you can capitalize on this economic reality by providing suitable content.

A story written for a weekly will resemble a news release, but you can spin it out for a few more paragraphs, adding extra detail. If you submit news stories suitable for print on a regular basis, a weekly newspaper in your coverage area may even ask you to write a regular column.

Checklist for generating media coverage

- hold a news conference

- conduct a poll

- write a news release

- write a "media advisory" to alert reporters that someone in your organization is available for interviews on a hot topic in the news

- write or ghostwrite an op-ed piece

- write a letter to the editor

- stage an event

- create a philanthropic tie-in to a program or event, such as food donation or contribution to a community-improvement project

- hold a town-hall meeting

- create an advisory group of citizen volunteers to contact the media about a specific event or cause related to your organization

- announce your employees' accomplishments such as publishing a book, testifying at hearings, inventing a new product, etc.

- hold a seminar or symposium for journalists with invited experts so they can learn more about your field

- write original news stories for short-staffed weeklies in your coverage area

- sign up for PRNewswire or Business Wire and submit your most appealing news and feature stories to them

- start a speaker's bureau

- explore "community access" or "public access" television; you may be able to produce original programming for cable TV that features your organization

CHAPTER SEVEN

SCORING POSITIVE PUBLICITY—PART II: WHEN *YOU* ARE THE EXPERT

CHAPTER 7:

Scoring Positive Publicity—Part II:
When *you* are the expert

When *you* are the expert, the key to a better publicity campaign is *more* articles, *more* quotes and *more* interviews. For maximum effectiveness, you need to get yourself into as many publications and on as many shows as possible. But every show and every publication is different. So how can one person with one product or service attract the attention of several media outlets? The answer is simple: a great hook.

Essentially, your hook is like a headline that makes someone want to read the whole story. It sparks an interest in the media outlet and influences them to publish or air your message to their audience. When push comes to shove, reporters and producers don't care about your business. They are only interested in how you can make their publication or show more appealing to their audience. Therefore, your hook should address the needs of a particular media outlet's readers or viewers. And each outlet you pitch should get its own unique hook congruent with its unique audience.

Adaptation is the foundation for creating your hook. Use these tips to develop your unique hook with each magazine, newspaper, and TV or radio show to get more interviews and more articles published:

Trick of the trade: An excellent resource that gives you an edge with the media is *Chase's Calendar of Events*. This book is published annually and lists scheduled events for every day of the year. For example, did you know that November 18th is Mickey Mouse's birthday, Prematurity Awareness Day, the Great American Smokeout, and Married to a Scorpio Support Day? Each day of the year has a list, so with a little creativity, you're bound to find something you can use. Editor's love anniversary dates like these. With a copy of *Chase's* on your shelf, you'll know what's happening beforehand, and you can develop your hook around an event, pseudo-event or commemoration. When you use these listings or adapt to other events in the news, you make your hook more appealing to the media.

Answer the question: Why are you different? Even though your business may be, say, personal investing or life planning or some other narrow field, chances are you know about a variety of other things. To get more press, you have to cover a broader range. What are your hobbies? Where did you grow up? How are you different from all the other business leaders? You participate in hundreds of different conversations with hundreds of different people about hundreds of different topics, and your input is valuable because of your specialization. You offer a unique perspective because of your background, so use this to your advantage as you develop a hook.

Sometimes, you must make small changes in your approach. For example, suppose you own a day spa and relaxation retreat. Everyone needs relaxation, whether they're at home or at work, so you can adapt this topic to fit almost anywhere. But the key is to adapt it for the publication. As we mentioned in Chapter 6, one author pitched several industry and trade publications with an article she had written around her subject titled "Take Six Months Off." No one bit with that hook. It turns out editors feared the reactions of executives who didn't want people in a work environment reading about sabbaticals! The tagline to the very same article became "Prevent Employee Burnout," and editors of business magazines appealing to CEOs loved it!

If something isn't working for you, keep an open mind and consider a different approach. When you talk with your media contacts or pitch your article ideas, adapt and expand your topic to fit their current needs, and you'll increase your exposure.

Always consider the audience when pitching and writing. Media professionals are concerned with only one thing: ratings, readership and hits. They want people to buy their magazine or tune into their show or "stick" on their Web site. And before they run your article or interview you they want to be sure you'll get attention. When you're pitching to the media, whether it is radio, print, Internet or television, you must think about what interests their audience, not about yourself. Imagine their perspectives, and base your hook on their needs. Think about what the readers of this magazine or the viewers of this show want to know. Why are they reading or watching in the first place? What problems do they have and how can you solve them?

Keep in mind that the same people read different publications for different reasons. For example, the CEO of a major corporation may read *Fast Company* and *The Wall Street Journal* at work on a regular basis to keep up with the latest economic trends. But at home, this CEO is a mother of two young children, so she also reads *Family Circle* for useable information about family health and easy recipes. Every night before bed, she likes to relax and read for entertainment, fashion ideas and beauty tips. Therefore, she also subscribes to *Vogue*. This woman reads a variety of publications for a variety of different reasons. So as you adapt your topic for a specific publication, think about who reads it and why. And don't forget: men read women's magazines, too. The more popular women's magazines, such as *Better Homes & Gardens*, draw more male readers than do male-targeted publications such as *Men's Health*.

Make a list of all the publications you'd like to appear in, and then think about the types of headlines you see on the covers. How can you make your topic fit within the interests of their readers? Next, brainstorm ideas for each publication. For example, suppose you are a public speaker, and the keynote speech you give addresses hormone imbalances, stress levels and chronic fatigue. You might want to consider the following pitches:

Woman's World:	How Stress Experts De-stress
Self Magazine:	Staying Healthy During Stressful Times
Parents Magazine:	When to Call a Doctor: Warning Signs for Kids
Wall Street Journal:	Reduce Stress at Work: Diet & Exercise Tips
Ladies Home Journal:	Tired All the Time? It Could Be Chronic Stress/Fatigue
Real Simple Magazine:	One-Month Health Makeover

These different hooks are all on the topic of stress; they are simply adjusted to fit the needs of each specific publication. The hooks address the audience directly and give them a reason for buying the magazine or watching the show.

As always, if you want to catch a fish, you have to use the right hook. Apply this same concept to your publicity campaign and develop a winning hook for each media outlet you approach. Expand your topic to appeal to more publications and more shows. With each outlet, adapt your hook to consider the audience's needs, because that's who the reporters and producers aim to please. Then link your topic to a current event to make it newsworthy. When you use these guidelines and create a winning hook, you will get more interviews, more articles published and more publicity for your career as an expert in your field, whether you are a doctor, lawyer, speaker or book author.

To show up on the news, you must be a consumer of news. Keep up with the times—and keep up with the *Times*! A vital aspect of a winning hook is newsworthiness. Media outlets love to have timely information linked to current events and trends. Exciting things happen every day all over the world: new products fill the market, technology develops advances, research draws conclusions and people make things happen. Start a habit of reading the newspaper and watching the news regularly, and then adapt your ideas to the most cutting-edge information.

For example, suppose you are a speaker or book author, and your area of expertise is circulatory health. Low-carb foods have been all over the news for some time, and a research team has just discovered a link between heart attacks and individuals who cut complex carbohydrates from their diets. Using your background in health, what does this mean for low-carb dieters? How does this new report affect the public? As an expert, you can answer these questions, so use this to your advantage. Mention the new research in your hook. Always know what's happening in the world, because if you can provide your unique take on a current event, the media will take notice.

Here are examples of a few PR/PR clients who landed in the national spotlight with the appropriate marriage of timing and subject matter:

- An explosion/a safety expert
- A Hollywood divorce/a relationship expert
- A disease scare/a health expert
- A high-profile lawsuit/ an attorney
- An important merger/a business strategist
- A new invention/a technology expert

Don't discount trade magazines. Niche publications are everywhere, and trade publications command wide audiences. Magazines exist that cater to the most narrow of enterprises, for example *Museum Stores, Auction World, Culinary Trends*. Most of these publications will allow you to submit an article you have written to them and others simultaneously. Relationship expert Karen Card reached a nice cross-section of America when her "All Work and No Dating" article was picked up by 21 publications including *Los Angeles Family, Virginia Engineer, Body Beautiful Magazine and Financial Services Advisor*. Sy Sperling's "Why Commercials Fail" was equally popular with a different crowd including *Commerce, Business Journal Online, Minorities & Women in Business* and *Broker Agent News*.

Time of year matters. Editors are always acutely aware of the season in which their publication hits the newsstands. They are working weeks and months ahead of schedule, deciding on their Christmas issue as early as the summer before. Again, target your pitches accordingly. If you want to be quoted as a health expert in a publication often read at the gym, remember that as summer approaches the female reader is less concerned about the cardio-health angle and more interested in the size of her thighs.

Here are just a few potential Springtime ideas from *Chase's* that can make an otherwise ho-hum pitch seem compelling and fresh:

As Young As You Feel Day—March 21
Injury Prevention Month—April
Stress Awareness Month—April
Workplace Conflict Awareness Month—April
Laugh at Work Week—April 1-7
National Networking Week—April 9-15
Administrative Professionals Week—April 22-28
Teen Self-Esteem Month—May
Women's Health Care Month—May
National Family Month—May

Whether your topic is management, health, motivation, or relationships, many of these special time periods can add extra pizzazz when you pitch a story to the media and offer yourself as an expert to interview. Take "Laugh at Work Week," for example. If you are a humorist, that's obviously a great title, but, if your topic is:

- Management, you can speak on how laughter increases productivity in the workplace
- Motivation, you can tie it in with positive thinking
- Medical, you can tie it into the endorphins that laughter releases

As an expert, you will benefit from the opportunity to write an op-ed piece. In Chapter 6, we outlined the winning elements of an op-ed piece, which runs on the page opposite the editorial page in the daily newspaper. What follows is an example of a piece that generated wide pickup in September 2006.

Why Women Need Katie Couric to Succeed

For decades, Americans have turned daily to the stoic comfort of their network anchors to watch history unfold. And even as viewers stray to the cable news channels' non-stop coverage of the sensational, for thirty minutes each day—and longer in times of crisis—network anchors still draw millions who seek the days' headlines from a familiar face.

Since television first entered our homes, those familiar faces who have sat solo in the anchor chair have been men. Each evening they arrived for work in their dark suit and appropriately matched tie, never having to worry that the next day's media cycle would include a critique of their hair color or length, or comment whether their outfit was too light or too dark, or whether it revealed too much or too little. And it would be inconceivable that relentless attention could be focused on the shape of their legs.

That will all change on September 5, when Katie Couric begins her role as the first woman to serve as the sole anchor of a major network news broadcast. One can only hope that her reporting of the day's news will be heard over the din that will inevitably follow focusing on her appearance and her personality.

Katie Couric may have shattered the glass ceiling of network news when she was selected to anchor without a male partner, but she is still frequently judged by the same separate—and biased—standards that other women face. Study after study demonstrates that women are evaluated more harshly than men and that unconscious stereotyping creates far greater hurdles for women seeking to advance in the workplace.

Consider the press coverage which followed the CBS announcement that Katie Couric would anchor the evening news broadcast. In the media frenzy that followed, nearly every article questioned whether she could demonstrate the necessary "gravitas" of an anchor after 15 years as the face of the Today Show. Yet when Tom Brokaw once made the same transition, it was without the accompanying media firestorm of doubts.

Nor have other male anchors faced such scrutiny. When Brian Williams ascended to the NBC anchor desk and Bob Schieffer commenced his service as interim CBS anchor, the coverage discussed their past roles in the news which had prepared them for their new position, without reference to their physique. Moreover, news stories referred to them by their last names, unlike the familiar media reference to "Katie," which only serves to undermine her role as a serious journalist. One commentator's words of wisdom included a recommendation that she cut her hair, avoid trendy outfits, and stop wearing earrings that dangle.

Most women recognize that Katie Couric is simply facing a very public version of what women in the workplace encounter each day. Be serious, but not stern. Be approachable, but not perky (a repeated description which must haunt Katie Couric in her dreams). Be aggressive, but not strident. Be sure to look good, but do not call undue attention to what you wear. If you are a working mom, be the perfect role model while walking the tightrope between commitment to the job and caring about your children. And do it all perfectly, because you will be judged to a higher standard. As working women know too well and as studies have confirmed, men are more likely to be judged on their potential, while women are judged on their performance.

As Katie Couric strives to succeed in what has been a distinctly male domain, women should be rooting for her success. She is undertaking a highly visible role where the examination will be relentless. After a decade and a half as the face of morning television, she will be entering into an entirely new relationship with her viewers. As in any relationship, that requires change and compromise. She will have to find a persona that is comfortable for her and her viewing audience. And she deserves some time to find that comfort zone. If she can successfully navigate the anticipated gauntlet of scrutiny and ultimately be judged on her competence, she will make it easier for other women who seek to break through gender barriers and be evaluated on their job performance.

In a world free of gender bias, we would not wake up on September 6 to detailed stories about Katie Couric's first broadcast which focus more on style than on substance. But we do not yet live in that world, so the media scrutiny will likely flourish in its analysis of her clothing, perkiness level, and whether she exuded the appropriate level of gravitas.

But like everything else she has done under the spotlight, Katie Couric can be expected to handle the glare with grace. That quality will serve as a positive role model for women everywhere who are striving to succeed in unfamiliar territory. Women need this success story to have a happy ending. And Katie Couric has earned it the old-fashioned way—by working hard and following her dreams.

Lauren Stiller Rikleen, author of *Ending the Gauntlet: Removing Barriers to Women's Success in the Law*, is the Executive Director of the Bowditch Institute for Women's Success and a senior partner in the law firm of Bowditch & Dewey, LLP.

Checklist for generating media coverage when you are the expert

- Send out a news release commenting on a recent poll

- write a "media advisory" to alert reporters you are available for interviews on a hot topic in the news

- write or ghostwrite an op-ed piece

- write a letter to the editor

- hook up with a local institution that is staging an annual event

- create a philanthropic tie-in by making a charitable donation of your speaker's fee

- volunteer to lend your expertise to an upcoming town-hall meeting

- announce your latest book, award, conference presentation or other accomplishment via news releases

- hold a seminar or symposium for journalists so they can learn more about your field

- write original news stories for short-staffed week-lies in your coverage area

- start your own newsletter, which the news media may then use for story ideas or even quote from

- join a speaker's bureau

CHAPTER EIGHT

HOLDING A NEWS CONFERENCE

CHAPTER 8:
Holding a News Conference

A news conference is a formal way to communicate with the news media. It has several advantages: it addresses the assembled media all at the same time, cuts off the public questioning at a clear ending point and generates interest in you or your organization or business. Most of all it signals the high importance of the subject matter.

Disadvantages include possible cynicism on the part of the reporters, who may develop the view that your news conference is "staged" or false news. You also risk marshaling your resources only to experience a no-show on the part of the media, especially if a large disaster in town draws all the camera crews away (it happens!). Another disadvantage is that the major content of the news conference must be kept quiet until the moment of its release, or the news value dissipates.

So the first order of business is to determine that the event is big enough to merit a news conference. Stories such as grand openings, new products or a new plant, mass hirings, discoveries, and collaborations among various entities in town are the sorts of things you might consider news conference-worthy.

In Chapter 6, we talked about the Moffitt Foundation and a local bank bombing when they staged a news conference to publicize a million-dollar donation to the Cancer Center. In addition to the news conference being held at the wrong time of day, the story had few fresh angles, and the donation was kept under such tight wraps that Moffitt's news professionals in PR-and-marketing department didn't know it was about to happen. Therefore the bank and the foundation lost the benefit of their expertise. So remember: more than almost any other method of generating publicity, the news conference requires planning and exquisite attention to detail.

Trick of the trade: Don't play favorites among reporters. Release all information at once during a news conference so that the media are competing on a level playing field. You might be tempted to favor one particular media news outlet, thinking you might generate greater story play in that one outlet or curry favor with a prominent reporter. However, you may alienate another reporter in the process. The risk isn't worth it. The news conference is a one-day story, while media coverage is an ongoing process that stretches into the future. Make your invitation list in advance and include print, television, Internet and radio reporters. Don't forget weekly and community newspapers. Make follow-up calls to encourage attendance.

Plan the location and logistics. When planning a news conference, choose a room or outdoor setting where TV news reporters will be able to line up side-by-side with enough space left over so print and radio reporters can sit near the front as well to see and hear. Decide whether you want a long table or a podium. Make sure there are adequate electrical receptacles. Do a "location scout" to ensure that the room is large and accessible enough. Sometimes news conferences are held outside, which holds advantages for TV crews who can use sunlight instead of setting up studio lighting. However, you must always have a plan B in case of bad weather.

A couple of days in advance, send out a media advisory announcing the date and time. Just before and during the news conference, the staff member whose phone number was on the media advisory should be answering the phone (or have someone covering it) so that reporters who are lost can be guided to the right place.

Decide whether you want to invite VIP guests such as the mayor or a prominent community citizen or author.

Assemble printed material. You will need collateral materials to go along with your news conference. You will want to have sheets that list the names and titles of anyone who will be speaking, including the person who introduces the main speaker. You might also consider providing a one-page sheet of bulleted information providing background on the topic. Facts, figures and charts—these are all great things to commit to paper.

Always have a stack of press kits on a nearby table, which should contain background information about your organization as well as copies of recent news clippings. Reporters from smaller organizations may not be as familiar with you as the reporters who cover you repeatedly.

Remember internal communications. Alert all of your employees that a news conference will occur so that they can feel part of this significant event. You may want to enlist your facilities and security departments, if your organization or business is large, to help with practical issues such as parking and setup for members of the media.

Enough staff people should be on hand to answer any questions or address any issues the media may have before or after the news conference. Those participating in the news conference should generally plan to hang around for one-on-one conversations with reporters at the conclusion of the event. It's helpful if the main players of your news conference are able to stay for approximately 30 minutes after the news conference to give exclusive soundbites or clarify any questions the reporters might have.

Know what to expect. In the case of newspapers and magazines, the reporter will probably arrive alone or perhaps with a photographer. Your local TV news station may cover the conference in various ways. They may send a complete crew including a reporter who will want to do his or her "standups" on the scene before leaving. Or they may simply entrust a videographer with capturing the pictures and sound needed. Later, during the broadcast, the anchor will introduce the story before scenes or soundbites from your news conference are played.

Sometimes a news conference is called for during a crisis. In this case, the procedure for setting up a news conference is identical. However, in addition, you may need to think through other potential scenarios. If you are a hospital where a celebrity patient died from a botched surgery, for instance, you will have several extra elements to consider, such as seeking permission to comment from the victim's family and shielding doctors and nurses from being accosted by reporters in the parking lots.

If the crisis involves a natural disaster or if privacy concerns prevail, the American Hospital Association's Society for Health-Care Strategy and Market Development suggests preparing an answer such as:

"That is all I can confirm at this time. We are very busy trying to deal with this situation, and we will need your patience for a short time. As soon as we have more information that has been confirmed, it will be disclosed to the public via the news media."

Be aware of deadlines. A mid-morning news conference may make the noon and 6 p.m. newscasts while giving newspaper reporters plenty of time to research their stories to meet their evening deadlines. Any hour later than 4 p.m. will create more of a scramble for both print and TV reporters, heightening the risk of sloppy or incomplete reporting. Good days for news conferences are Tuesdays and Wednesdays, and midmorning is a good time.

Media train everyone who will appear before the cameras. Answers should be relatively brief and to the point, addressing the questions asked. As always in an interview, it's OK to say, "I don't know but will get that answer for you." If your CEO, say, is holding a news conference, make sure one or two key staff members are on hand to take over the microphone, providing needed background or detail. This CEO should stick to statements of policy and big-picture values, while other managers can fill in facts and figures.

Eye contact is important in a news conference. If you are not seasoned, you may be tempted to shift your eyes between cameras or cameras and reporters. This may be appropriate behavior in "real life" but makes you look insecure and shifty when played and replayed. Always look at the reporter and remember that you are having a conversation.

Anticipate the obvious questions that will be asked so that you will be able to quote facts and figures, speaking from a posture of confidence and authority.

Go over the techniques outlined in previous chapters about bridging and fielding tough questions in case a reporter decides to be aggressive. Also don't let yourself be distracted by naïve or even amazing questions, because sometimes a city editor or assignment editor will not want to spare a veteran reporter to cover a staged event. He or she may be inclined to send a rookie instead.

Dress should follow the rules for TV—solid colors, nothing distracting about jewelry or hair. Open, relaxed body language should be rehearsed ahead of time to appear natural. Remember that people draw their lasting conclusions from body language and tone of voice more than they do from the actual words that are spoken.

Provide visuals for the TV cameras. These can be props, colorful graphs or flip charts. Also plan on providing opportunities for B-roll to be shot, such as people in your institution at work or the principals of the news conference walking to and from their offices.

The large poster board behind you makes a good prop. It can summarize the points you want to discuss. The poster board eliminates the need for a script or a list of bullet points. It also creates a more interesting photograph that editors are likely to choose for their broadcasts or page layouts.

If possible, have one or two "outside" people related to the story on hand for interviews. These can be the clients, customers, constituents or stakeholders. The media love case studies and anecdotes. Having outside people available will enable reporters to efficiently round out their stories and to cover the basics of their newsgathering tasks before they leave the premises. In that way, you will gain the advantage of creating extra time for them to get back to you with further questions they may have.

Don't work from prepared statements. Some CEOs insist on having their messages drafted in advance. This is a mistake. Some rehearsal is appropriate. But the best communicators use only bullet points to keep them on track. That way, their communications are spontaneous, authoritative and authentic, never monotonous, scripted or dull. Make sure you open the news conference by putting the event into perspective—explaining why the news was important enough to merit a formal announcement.

Create a timetable and announce it in advance. Welcome the reporters and thank them for coming. Let the reporters know how much time you are dedicating to the news conference, including time for questioning. Have someone assigned to the task of closing down the news conference, perhaps by saying, "we have time for just one more question, as Dr. So-and-so must get back to his or her surgeries."

Before ending the news conference, thank the reporters for coming. Later, send thank-you notes to the reporters who attended.

Checklist for planning a news conference

- phone the media in advance to see who plans to attend, both to aid your preparations and to increase the comfort level of those who will be facing the reporters

- make sure you have not left any media outlets off your list, including radio reporters or freelancers

- if you work for a research or medical institution, doublecheck the publication date of any journal article to make sure you are not violating embargoes

- arrange for your own videotaping if possible to create your own record of the event

- do a run-through if time permits, practicing answers to tough questions and becoming comfortable with graphics to be shown

- don't leave media notification to chance; use fax, phone and e-mail to alert them to the news conference

- if you are seeking broad coverage, hold the news conference between 9 a.m. and 10 a.m. or, if afternoon is necessary, between 1:30 p.m. and 2:30 p.m.

- have a podium in place for your people to stand and for the electronic media to position their microphones

- arrange for audio box and sound system for reporters' microphones

- give the news media as much notice as possible without jeopardizing the news value of the conference through premature leaks

- keep a log of the reporters and news organizations who attend

CHAPTER
NINE

PREPARING FOR AN INTERVIEW

CHAPTER 9:
Preparing for an Interview

Reporters gather information for their stories by doing an interview or interviews. Print stories need quotes from the people involved; broadcast stories need soundbites. Reporters will make judgments about you based on how you handle the interview. The public will draw conclusions based on what you say and how you say it.

If you give a good interview, writers will contact you for story after story. At PR/PR, proven methods of gaining media exposure lead to clients being quoted in national magazines time after time. This is true even for people who are not household names. For instance, *Cosmopolitan, Redbook*, the *New York Times* and dozens of other publications interviewed and quoted Barbara Hemphill, author of *Taming the Paper Tiger*. Jason Jennings, author of *Less Is More*, was quoted in more than 40 magazines and interviewed on scores of radio programs.

Do you know what it's like to talk to boring people? They drone on for hours about topics that don't interest you, and all you can think about is getting rid of them. Keep this in mind when you talk to the media, because if you're boring, they won't want to talk with you ever again. But if you have energy and keep your responses on the topic, you'll keep the media professionals interested.

Psychological research shows that people conclude more from your tone of voice and even from your body language than they do from your actual words. Even if the interview does not involve a media crisis, self-interest still dictates that you not waste a reporter's time or create a bad impression. To paraphrase a title about old age, interviews are not for sissies. Be prepared.

Make sure your content is sharp and to the point. You can do this by anticipating a reporter's questions. Ask the reporter what the story is about. If the subject is, say, how your community spends its charity dollars, and you work for a nonprofit agency, expect questions about your agency's budget and clientele. Be ready with numbers, such as how many people you serve each year, and with facts, such as where those populations are based. Also have stories to tell that play up your agency's mission. Come up with a human-interest anecdote, and the reporter will almost certainly bite.

Think through what your audience cares about. What concerns them? Refine your message. By familiarizing yourself with popular publications within your audience, you should gain an understanding of what issues are important to them and what interests them. Define the lasting impression you wish to make on the public. Then marshal your facts and figures. Gather your anecdotes accordingly.

Incorporate personal experiences into your responses. As political consultant James Carville says, the human brain is "hardwired" for stories. Tell stories. Audiences love to hear firsthand accounts of experiences relating to the topic. It helps them feel as if they know you personally. But make sure you stay on topic, and don't get distracted with your story.

Eliminate jargon and keep sentences short. Even complex ideas are best explained in short, simple sentences. Keep sentence construction simple (subject-verb-object). Paint word pictures. Speak in concrete images that create images in people's minds.

Trick of the trade: Adjust your style depending on whether you are dealing with broadcast or print. When talking with print reporters, speak slowly enough for them to take notes. Do not be disconcerted because they are writing down what you say. Repeat your main points during the interview. To deal effectively with an on-camera reporter, keep your answers relatively short—more crisp and punchy. The average sound bite may run less than 20 seconds. The camera can literally flatten you, so project extra energy to convey commitment and feeling. When giving a radio interview over the phone, stand up. This will project extra energy. Remember that television is a medium of emotion. A talking head is a stuffed shirt. The person who conveys emotion, passion and belief has the best chance of being remembered.

Solve the writer's problems. When it comes to stories, each reporter and producer has a unique personality and unique needs. If you can figure out what the reporters want, you make their jobs much easier. And when you make a media professional's job easier, he or she will come back to you for more quotes and more interviews. So ask the reporters what other stories they're researching and for what other publications they write. Ask how you can help them and what other topics they'd like to see. Let the reporters, editors and producers know that you care about their stories and their audiences. In this way, you are taking the interview opportunity and transforming it into the chance to establish a rapport and working relationship with a media professional.

The key to effective preparation is preparing your messages. Make a list of the most important points you would like the reporter to grasp. He or she is the person who will filter your story to the public. When sitting down to write, he or she will be faced with myriad quotations and facts—from you and from all his or her other sources. You want what you have said to remain paramount. Cross all but the most vital three messages off of your list. If possible, work with only two.

Come up with facts, figures and stories that bolster these points. What if the reporter doesn't ask you about them? Master the art of the "bridge." (Read on.)

In deciding on your main messages, think of TV commercials and other messages beamed at you throughout the day. Which do you remember? Those with compelling images, emotional content and a main message. Advertising agencies don't make millions by being all over the map. They focus, focus, focus. So can you. Avoid the temptation to say everything about your company or book or product. Refrain from providing exhaustive lists of facts, dwelling on company history or release documents designed only to make powerful board members or corporate officials look good.

Concentrate on your key messages and illustrative anecdotes. Keep in mind that you want to be quotable. Don't be too wordy. Guard against going off on tangents. Concentrate on the substance you wish to convey rather than the product you are pushing. (This holds true even if the product is yourself!) Reporters are always on guard against being hyped or being used as a promotion vehicle. So don't be pushy about what you want, because they may or may not have room in their story to mention your product or service. But if you ask nicely, you'll have a better chance of getting it mentioned. Excessive promotion is a huge turnoff.

The art of bridging will take you far. You should always endeavor to answer a reporter's question to the extent that you can. However, your goal is to leave your audiences with recall of your key messages. You need to repeat your two to three main points during the interview. Bridge phrases will allow you to do this.

After you have answered the reporter's question directly and briefly or explained why you cannot, immediately transition to your key messages. Do this with phrases that become turning points. For example, "let me just add." Or "that's a vital point because..." Even "what is most important for your viewers (or readers) to understand is..." Or "I'd like to go back to the point about..."

These bridge phrases allow you to turn the conversation back to your key points with ease. Practice phrases that will help you bridge from a reporter's question to a key message you wish to convey. You can come up with bridge phrases of your own.

On TV, appearance counts. Because innocent mannerisms can make you seem evasive or flakey, you need to give appearance and body language some thought before going on camera. Media professionals wear powder on camera because hot lights make the skin shine in an unflattering, distracting way. The look of sweat can also make it seem as though the reporter has struck a nerve or put you on the hot seat. Apply powder in a shade that matches your skin tone before going on camera. It's okay to ask the reporter if you look too oily before starting the interview. He or she is well accustomed to this question.

Wear solid-colored clothing, avoiding colorful prints or plain white. Women should avoid jewelry that is too dangly or flashy. Hair should frame the face, not distract from the message. Your wardrobe should reflect where you work or the image you are trying to portray.

Keep your body language open. Pay attention and look engaged. Don't fidget or swivel around in your chair or cross your arms. This behavior can make you seem nervous or defensive.

Be assertive and direct, and frame your answers in a positive way. Speak in complete thoughts. Take control of your nerves, or you are likely to forget your key messages.

Ignore the camera or any other distraction. Speak to the reporter. Imagine you are speaking to an audience of one single person such as your Aunt Bess. This mental trick will help you relax and connect with the audience.

If you expect to represent yourself or your company repeatedly on camera, seek media training. Even seasoned CEOs can stutter and become self-conscious (or, on the flip side, appear abrasive and arrogant) when the camera starts to roll. On-camera practice will put you at ease.

Plan what to do if you feel distressed during the interview. A number of steps can help you get past an uncomfortable moment and turn a potential blunder into a score. If you freeze for any reason, ask the reporter to repeat the question. This will give you more time to organize a response. If you don't have all the information at hand to respond fully, feel free to immediately turn to your staff or others within the organization to provide details. Reporters won't resent interruptions if it means they leave the interview with all of the information they need to write their stories.

If you have had advance notice of the interview, you might want to have charts and graphs on hand or a list of bullet points to help educate the reporter on the topic. Do not load him or her down with annual reports, articles embedded in thick magazines or hundreds of pages of computer printouts unless they've requested all that. (The exception to this is when you are compelled to release information you hope the reporter won't find, in which case you bury it in hundreds if not thousands of pages. Do not try this tactic without professional help.)

Unless you are on live TV, if you are really unhappy with the way you have begun to answer a question, simply stop. It's fine to start over because the tape will be edited back at the studio. This tactic may not work with a print reporter, who may choose your original phrasing over the version you have attempted to refine. If you start out on the wrong foot with a print reporter, it's better to say something like, "wait, what I said is not quite accurate. A more accurate way to describe the situation is..." Stress the word "accurate," which will force the reporter into a shady ethical area if he or she chooses your earlier rendition.

Be relaxed, flexible and spontaneous. Given all of the preparation you have done for the interview, you may be tempted to parrot a canned response. Don't. Canned responses are deadly. They communicate your inability to think on your feet. They also imply that you are so uptight about the situation that you fear speaking about it in a normal way. That posture hardly conveys a confident attitude.

The reporter is interviewing you because you have information in your brain or at your fingertips. You are the authority, the source. You have mastery of the subject. Your credibility will come across the more you can relax and be yourself.

Some media trainers recommend a slight pause before answering a question on tape. A rush to answer sometimes seems too push-button, as though you could not wait to spill out your programmed response. Pausing also conveys the image that you are considering the question, even though, through careful preparation, you know exactly the message you intend to convey.

Never repeat the negative word or phrase that may show up in a reporter's question. A reporter will almost always feed you a word they wish for *you* to repeat back in your answer. That way they can quote you making the judgment call rather then undertaking the rhetorical acrobatics it will require to do it themselves while still conveying proper journalistic objectivity.

Answer questions in complete thoughts, but frame those thoughts in your own words.

Remember that the interview is a business transaction, and exchange of information is the goal. In most cases the reporter is not out to get you or to manufacture conflict (although he or she will certainly play the conflict up). He or she is merely doing the job. Your job is to position yourself to come across in ways that best further the reason you are giving the interview in the first place!

If you prepare yourself to make a polished impression, you can exert a measure of control of your nerves—and your message. The interview is not an exercise to be feared but rather a process to help reach the public with mutually beneficial information exchange.

Skilled, confident communicators are a joy to watch. They convey emotion and resist the news reporter's or anchor's attempts to steer them into unpleasant places. With spontaneity, they speak directly to the question asked. Then, without any but the media-savvy even realizing it, they bridge to a repetition of their own key messages. They don't look robotic or trained.

They look caring and smart. They communicate all of these elements through tone of voice, body language and word choice.

These tactics and techniques are not aptitudes you are born with. They are honed skills that can be learned and practiced by virtually anyone in the media spotlight.

Interviews are a great subject for lifelong learning. Preparing for an interview is important. Every person who at some point may face a news camera can benefit greatly from rehearsal and practice, preferably in front of a camera with someone playing the part of a reporter to make the scenario as realistic and edgy as possible. Continue your media training for life by evaluating your real on-camera performances and those of your colleagues.

The many guest-hungry radio programs afford a great opportunity for publicity. Although radio interviews usually only entail a 10-minute phone call, you still need to take your time and prepare for it beforehand.

Besides spreading the word about your product or service, what's the best thing about landing a radio interview? You can conduct the interview wearing your pajamas! But there's a catch. You can't *sound* like you're wearing your pajamas. Even though you're talking on the phone to the reporter and no one can see you, you still have to communicate a professional image. Otherwise, the radio producers might bump you from the show, and they definitely won't call you back for future stories.

So how can you ensure that you make the right impression and, perhaps more important, that you're called back for more interviews? You can use the following 10 tips for giving great radio interviews:

1. **Allow yourself private time prior to the interview.** Use this time to relax and focus. Imagine that you are speaking with the interviewer face to face. Rehearse the points you want to make and remember that you can never be too prepared.

2. **Seek a quiet spot for the interview.** If you are speaking from home, close yourself off in a room with few distractions. Turn off your computer, TV or radio, and clear your desk so nothing can take your mind off the conversation.

3. **Write your main points before the call begins.** Do not read scripted responses from a preprinted sheet, because reporters and show hosts can tell when something is being read to them versus when you're giving honest answers. But do prepare a notecard with three to five topics you would like to touch upon during the interview. That way you won't struggle with an answer during the interview.

4. **Show that you care about the reporter and his or her story.** Be helpful and responsive to the reporter's requests. Before going on live or live-to-tape, ask the interviewer what you can do to make his or her job easier. Then really listen to his or her answer and be an eager, accessible source of information.

5. **Stand while giving the interview.** Even though you're talking on the phone, act as if you were giving a live presentation and stand tall. Standing will raise your energy level, and you will be more alert than if you were sitting. Radio interviewers love energy and can pick up on your mood.

6. **Smile and answer honestly and sincerely.** People can hear your smile over the phone and a reporter will feel

more comfortable after hearing the joy in your voice. Also, the sound of smiling builds a rapport with interviewers. If they feel they can trust you, they will think of you first for their next interview.

7. **Put energy and spunk into your voice.** No one wants to listen to a monotonous drone on the radio, and the reporters and producers know this. So even before the interview, assure the radio reporters that you'll be pleasant to the listeners' ears by putting energy into your voice. This could make the difference between a mundane interview and a great conversation.

8. **Have backup information handy.** Reporters will inevitably ask you one question you don't want to or can't answer (this is another place your notecard comes in handy). In case you are unable to respond, you can say, "That brings up an interesting point..." then go on to one of your notecard points, as described in the "bridge" section above. Or offer to find out the answer to the questions and get back to them as soon as possible.

9. **Be forthright.** Answer the reporter's question accurately and thoroughly, and don't be afraid to give away too much information. Many business professionals fear that they might give too much and then no one will buy their product or service. But it's impossible to spoil years of experience and training in a five-minute radio interview, and the radio listeners will actually want more after you add value to their lives. So answer the questions. Never say, "You'll find the answer to that when you buy my product or service."

10. **Use the word "you" often.** The word "you" draws the listeners in and helps them relate to what you're saying. And always give the listeners a reason to pay attention by articulating the benefits to the listener of the facts in your presentation.

Checklist of things to learn from a reporter before any interview.

- Name of reporter

- News organization

- Basic outline or angle of the story

- The reporter's deadline

- Other information the reporter would like you to have on hand (documents, charts, etc.)

- Any particular questions you need to research so you will have the answer on hand

- List of other potential sources for this story (just remember the reporter is not obligated to provide this information to you)

- Contact information for the reporter, e-mail as well as phone number

- Reminder to yourself to give the reporter your after-hours contact information. You never know when the story is going into production or which editors may have last-minute questions.

CHAPTER TEN

WHEN CRISIS HITS:
10 RULES FOR IMMEDIATE RESPONSE

CHAPTER 10:

When Crisis Hits:
10 rules for immediate response

Do you know the No. 1 best way to keep headlines about you and your company positive?

Do you know what body language can make you look like a liar on camera—even when you're telling the truth?

Have you ever done an interview with a news reporter? Did you prepare? How?

Can you explain why truth (not Stephen Colbertesque *truthiness*) could be vital to your company's bottom line? To your survival on the job, even at the top?

Are you prepared to immediately respond if crisis hits, preserving your reputation and your organization's focus on its mission?

If you are employed virtually anywhere in America, these questions pertain to the performance of your job, as well as to your personal and professional success. Even though daily newspapers are in decline, weeklies are on the rise. Television news can create a legend or a scapegoat in an instant. Internet blogs and podcasts wield influence. (Few leaders can withstand a morass of messy headlines; even CBS news anchor Dan Rather fell prey to bad publicity about questionable reporting and sloppy editing.) No retailer nor entrepreneur, no speaker nor author nor small businessperson can survive in the marketplace without the top-of-mind awareness news coverage creates.

There is no city small enough, no business obscure enough to claim freedom from the media's influence. Even houses patched up with duct-tape will have a television set. Public libraries are filled with people using the Internet, not to mention millions of people on home or school computers. For people who cannot afford a newspaper, free newspapers abound. There is virtually no way, at least legally, to keep the media from covering you if they decide you are a story. You can be the smallest nonprofit agency, a sole proprietor or the head of a giant company. Whatever your role, you could end up in the news. (And, of course, sometimes you want to end up in the news—as often as possible. As author Gore Vidal says, never say no to either sex or an invitation to be on television.)

Although no one is immune from crisis that can take away earning power, sully a reputation or distract from a mission, a media crisis doesn't have to mean prosecutors lead away a company's handcuffed CEO. A media crisis exists when news coverage reaches an intensity that distracts from the mission. Reporters facing instant deadlines will go with what they've got. They won't wait hours or days for you or the organization to craft the appropriate response. They are writing and reporting even as you strategize and stew, create talking points, clear statements with your lawyers and debate who the best company spokesman would be. If you aren't available, the reporter will move on to other sources to find answers ... sources whose output you cannot control.

If a crisis is occurring, why should you care what the news media think? Public perception allows you or your organiza-

tion to operate within the outer world of your clients or constituents, not to mention shareholders, stakeholders or customers.

A scandal at the Walter Reed Army Medical Center
resulted in the firing of not just the general running the hospital, but also the resignation of the man at the top: Army Secretary Francis J. Harvey. The scandal involved the poor quality
treatment of outpatient veterans at the hospital. Just days
before Harvey's ouster in March 2007, *Army Times* printed a
story saying that soldiers had been forbidden to speak to the
media ("Walter Reed Patients Told to Keep Quiet"). Squelch-
ing the soldiers was just one more negative factor that a media
savvy approach would have avoided. Headlines can be lethal,
as the general and the army secretary learned, and attempts to
overcontrol can only make things worse. Consider the statements of Defense Secretary Robert M. Gates at the army secretary's ouster (*The New York Times* headlined the story "Army
Secretary Is Ousted in Furor Over Hospital Care"):

"I am disappointed that some in the Army have not ade-
quately appreciated the seriousness of the situation. Some have
shown too much defensiveness and have not shown enough
focus on digging into and addressing the problems."

Beyond your own personal comfort in keeping your job,
consider the economic costs to your company or organization
of poor public perceptions. How you handle a media crisis can
influence current and future relationships with customers and
constituencies of all types. Some companies (think ValuJet
after a fiery crash and subsequent disclosure of repeated safety
violations) have even decided to abandon their names because
publicity was so bad.

If you remember just one thing, remember this. A govern-
ing reality of the media crisis may be hard to grasp, but it is

fundamental. Whatever the crisis or its causes, the crisis itself is not the lasting issue. The lasting issue is how you and your organization respond to the crisis. Do the right thing, and your image will take care of itself.

Image is reality. How many companies and CEOs have learned that sad lesson after-the-fact? Consider Enron or Arthur Andersen. Any business or organization, no matter its size, can be caught up in disastrous news coverage that can, at worst, bring down the company or, at best, distract from the mission.

The bad news is you cannot change the reality. The good news is you can learn strategies to keep your company's image pristine (and your job or profits safe!) even in the midst of crisis. Even if you are not thoroughly conversant with the intricacies of dealing with the news media, you can become media trained with a little study. You can enhance your reputation, reach new markets, achieve personal and professional goals, all with the greater fame and credibility that attach to media coverage. You can use the power of the media to advance your career—even, ironically during times of crisis.

So let's go back to our first question above.

The No. 1 best way to keep headlines about you and your company positive is *simple*. And yet it must not be easy, because time and time again even the biggest companies break all the rules, predictably jettisoning themselves and their organizations in the process.

Ready for the secret of how to create a stellar image with the news media and keep it that way?

Be true to your mission. Be transparent. Tell the truth.

Take care of the substance of your work, and your image will take care of itself.

The public understands that people are human and humans make mistakes. On the flip side, the public won't forgive or forget callousness, corruption or abuse of power—which cover-ups always imply. The greater your understanding of what motivates the news media, the more adept you can be at generating news coverage that creates a lasting positive impression with the public.

> **Trick of the trade:** Everyone has a job to do in a crisis, including members of the media. Expect courtesy. But don't take it personally if not everyone behaves becomingly at all times. TV's fictional detectives can tell TV's abrasive reporters to buzz off. You can't. Whoever is speaking to the media on behalf of the organization must project sensitivity, sincerity, a commitment to calm diplomacy—even humbleness.

Do you know how to best respond if crisis hits? Remember tone. When speaking about the situation, convey concern, care and empathy. The audience will soak up the genuineness (or lack thereof) of your caring by what you say and how you say it. Sometimes this means making a sincere expression of regret. If the public believes that you care about your employees, the public interest and anyone your company has hurt directly or indirectly, then the public will believe what you say.

Present the facts. Disclose as fully as you are able. Reassure the public, the news media and your company's employees that the situation is under control. If laws or policies prohibit sharing full information, spell those laws or policies out. Always articulate the big view, the greater good. Have those phrases ready.

Be aware that the company's legal counsel may be operating under outmoded precepts. "No comment" was once the standard single utterance approved by lawyers. Lawyers understandably quake at the thought of statements that might jeopardize the company in a future lawsuit. However, this is old-school thinking. As Enron showed us, there may not be a company left to defend by the time a case gets to court. In any event, losing in the court of public opinion can guarantee a catastrophe at trial.

If your company has made a blunder, express commitment to finding the causes and putting steps in place to prevent recurrence. Resist the temptation to employ passive-voice construction. This rule is universal and is crucial in crisis-communications situations. For instance, do not say, "mistakes were made." Say, "we made mistakes." Stay away from jargon as well. Use plain English.

If appropriate, articulate the company's mission statement to demonstrate what's most important in the situation, to create perspective and to end interviews and sound bites on a positive note.

Can you explain the relationship of truth (not truthiness) to your bottom line? Image is reality. Yet even the largest companies insist on learning that lesson over and over, humiliated in front of our eyes. If only they would tell the truth, as quickly and fully as possible. How many years, for instance, will it take the coal-mining industry to overcome the impression of callousness and disregard for human life created during the Sago mine disaster?

Truthiness, by contrast, is associated with spin. Reporters can smell spin a mile away. The public is more sophisticated these days when it comes to detecting BS, stonewalling or evasion. The news media suffer bouts of unpopularity, to be sure, but that fact cuts you no break. The media remain the most important vehicle, conveyer and filter of your image to masses of people.

The most successful CEOs in our country understand that a company's every major step requires a keen understanding of public reaction and a gift for generating public support. Think of the speed with which Jet Blue announced a Passenger's Bill of Rights after being skewered in the news media for abusing passengers with hours-long waits on the tarmac. The most gifted CEOs understand that the best communications function is one that is integrated into the company's strategic decision-making.

If your company or organization is large, you should have a crisis-communications plan in place. Whether you have such a plan, no matter its detail, here are 10 rules for immediately responding to a crisis.

1. **In all public statements, focus on the bottom line of what you want the audience to be made to understand.** In a crisis, even experienced members of the communications team can allow their anxiety to take them off on tangents. They may wring their hands over how board members or other important stakeholders will respond. They may become nervous Nellies over the prospect of lawsuits or bold headlines. Forget about all that for the moment.

   The goal is to come up with the words, *now*, that will bring the public to the understanding you desire. You might even want to take a blank sheet of paper, draw a circle and write "bottom line of audience" in the center. Draw spokes and label them "proof." For each spoke, come up with a story, example, statistic or fact that proves the single most important message you wish your audience to understand.

The team, or a subset of the team, should be crafting these anecdotes, marshaling these facts and figures, and refreshing themselves on the organization's stories that are relevant to the crisis at hand. There is no time for digression or displays of internal corporate politics.

During interviews, never allow a reporter to anger or goad you. Never walk out on an interview. Stay cordial.

2. **Whatever information will eventually come out, make sure you release it immediately.** Your instinct may be to hold back, circle the wagons, hunker down. But remember, the media are like birds on a wire. One lands there, and before you know it the wire is full. If reporters morph into full-blown competitive mode, each will be trying to outdo the other by ferreting out facts the others have missed.

If only one newspaper breaks the story—and more than one daily circulates in your city or region—expect the others to follow with stories of their own. If the crisis at hand could bring negative publicity to you or your organization, your goal should be to let all the unflattering details come out at once. That way the story will be confined to a single day with no justification for media outlets to dredge it up again. One bad story is far easier to weather than weeks or months of constant reminders. Worse, a continuing story is far more likely to spread like a forest fire, breaking local boundaries and coming to life in the national media as well.

(A fascinating footnote: the "information dump" technique is also called the Kissinger rule, as Dr. Henry Kissinger articulated this concept during Watergate.)

3. **There's nothing wrong with saying "I don't know."** Don't panic if a news reporter asks a question you don't know the answer to. You may feel that you have been caught off guard, that you *should* know the answer. As always, honesty is the best policy. Acknowledge any gaps in your determining of the facts, but pledge to seek out accurate information. You can say, "Let me get back to you when I have more information."

Present the facts, offer reassurances that the situation is under control and spell out how the crisis is being addressed. Finally, remind the reporter that steps are in place to determine the cause of the crisis and guarantee that unfortunate event won't happen again.

4. **Never forget the media will imply that someone is the "bad guy."** Go into hunker-down mode and that someone can be you. Why do some companies look better after a crisis and others look worse?

Because Johnson & Johnson recalled and destroyed 31 million bottles of Tylenol and came out six weeks later with a tamper-resistant package, the company maintained a pristine image. Its crisis-communications plan articulated the highest value: protecting the public interest. The company's CEO went on camera and took ownership of the situation, expressing empathy for the victims.

A second 1980s classic case study, by contrast, involves the Exxon Valdez oil spill. A company vice president accused the news media of sensationalizing the story. On national television, millions of Americans were watching seals and oil-coated birds die agonizing deaths. The company's president didn't bother to board a corporate jet to visit the scene in the immediate aftermath. As environmentalists bathed the birds and fishermen struggled to support their families in the ruined waters, company leaders appeared worse than callous. Decades later, the phrase "Exxon Valdez" creates horrific pictures in the minds of those who remember watching those oil-soaked birds.

A more recent case in point: During sweeps coverage on television news, some investigative reporters for television followed up on stories that ran in major newspapers across the country about hospital-induced infections. Your risk of getting a nosocomial infection at some hospitals is scandalously high. Sometimes high infection rates arise because of improper procedures, laziness or carelessness. Who will be the bad guy in this story? If you are running the hospital, you have a choice. If you stonewall or mislead the media, the bad guy will be you. If you are open, truthful and exude compassion for the public, the bad guy will be those nasty microbes that make people sick—even if your hospital has been the site of an unfortunate incident. (Say, a nurse with inch-long fake nails carrying bugs from patient to patient.)

5. **Put your lawyer's advice in perspective.** In the example of Johnson & Johnson above, the company's CEO listened to his lawyers' advice—and then rejected it. In a crisis, legal review is a given. It is a lawyer's job to protect the company from lawsuits or, if a case goes to court, win them. What's more, corporate behavior can sometimes lead to criminal charges.

Despite the attorney's legitimate role in plotting out crisis communications, old-school legal thinking can create damage to reputation that may never be undone. Of course, if no statements are put out there in the public domain, then no statements can be twisted around later at trial. The flaw in this thinking is that the world has changed. An individual or corporation can become so bloodied during a media frenzy that, at trial, there is literally no corporate entity left to defend.

The media operate under their own sets of rules. Strategies that make for a winning trial outcome can lead to disaster in the court of public opinion.

Find the best way to incorporate lawyers into your crisis-communications team. Either they can provide constructive assistance in crafting messages during the writing process, or they may work better when presented with drafts of statements they can review and edit.

6. **Never say "no comment."** The public hears this as the universal admission of guilt. If you are caught in a situation where federal laws or other considerations mandate that you keep silent on key elements of the crisis, then find something that *can* be said. Reiterate your commitment to openness and transparency. If state or federal law, business practices or client privacy issues prevent you from fully answering a particular question, spell out your willingness to help the reporter gain the full story but be explicit about why you must hold back information. Remain accessible to news reporters.

7. **Convey concern, care, empathy and a commitment to the public interest.** Speak in plain English. No jargon or legalese should show up in your sound bites or quotes given to news reporters. Remember that the public is judging you, making key decisions about whether to trust you

in the future, by how you are treating anyone your company may have victimized.

Practice phrases and techniques to help deal with tough or hostile questions from reporters. The phrases include, "another thing to remember is..." and "while the point you make is important, let me add ..." As you form your answers, your techniques can include becoming more adamant in your response, offering documentation and giving out the names of other sources who can substantiate what you have said.

Well before the crisis hits, make sure you have practiced preparing for and giving interviews. Media training is widely available, including on-camera components to give you feedback about expressions, tone of voice, phrasing and body language.

8. **Remember the power of apology.** Apology has traditionally been the anathema of attorneys. However, recent studies have shown that hospitals that own up to their mistakes and apologize suffer fewer lawsuits. Colorado and Oregon have passed laws saying an apology cannot be used in court to help convict a doctor of malpractice.

"At some medical schools, including Vanderbilt University School of Medicine in Nashville, courses in communicating errors and apologizing now are mandatory for medical students and residents," reports *The Wall Street Journal*. "Insurers across the nation, including General Electric Co.'s giant Medical Protective unit, are beginning to urge clients to acknowledge errors and apologize."

What is true in the medical industry applies to other companies as well. Consider the speed with which JetBlue's

CEO David G. Neeleman issued not only apologies but also a Passenger's Bill of Rights after customers were mistreated.

9. **Tell the truth.** News reporters are excellent at detecting lies, and news cameras are even better. In any event, the truth has a way of coming out. First anticipate what the reporter will ask. What's more, make sure you list those questions you least wish to acknowledge, the ones that make your stomach churn. Even though it may seem counterintuitive, prepare an answer to each that is on point.

Why "counterintuitive"? The human affinity for denial. You might have the impulse, or your lawyer may issue the instruction, to rationalize the tough question away. A second case in point: In dealing with a media crisis, a medical institution in Tampa convinced itself during high-level discussions that it had *not* violated one of its own policies, which had led to a grave mishap involving scores of patients. A reporter's quick check of a state regulatory department found that it had, in fact, violated a key internal policy. Of course that violation was detailed and highlighted in the story, in a way that implied the institution had attempted to deceive the newspaper (and, by extension, the public). Avoid the temptation to give into denial. Be scrupulously honest.

10. **Do the right thing.** In the aftermath of a crisis, you or your organization can take the opportunity to reestablish trust. Trust-building comes about when companies consistently take the high road. Here are three quick examples of companies that could have done it better.

Consider FEMA director Mike Brown, remembered for his fixation on his choice of clothing rather than compassion for Katrina victims in New Orleans. In a storm of publicity, he resigned within weeks after the hurricane hit. In a crisis, people expect leadership. They expect the president of Exxon to show up at the scene, expressing sympathy and outlining concrete steps to prevent another disaster. They expect the head of FEMA to move heaven and earth to get water to thirsty families in public shelters.

When a jury awarded a widow $250 million in damages against Merck, the size of the damage award suggested jury outrage at the pharmaceutical company's behavior. "It was a failure by Merck to communicate risk that the jury in Texas punished," writes Paul Holmes, an expert in reputation management.

In January 1996, after eliminating 40,000 jobs, AT&T focused more on the approval of Wall Street and less on the reaction of the public (which was, after all, primed to expect stories of worker insecurity and corporate greed). Dick Martin, former vice president of public relations at AT&T, now says that he and others on the communications team missed the symbolism of the event.

The layoffs had come as part of AT&T's divestiture of Lucent and NCR. AT&T tried to do the right thing by providing job-placement assistance to the laid-off employees. It didn't matter. The company's stock increased, but negative publicity intensified. "As it turned out, we had focused too much on the newspapers tucked into the seat pockets in our executives' limousine," Martin writes. "We should have paid more attention to the evening news broadcasts, which were how most people across the country heard about our downsizing."

You may be tired of dealing with the media after a crisis, but it's vital that your company be visible, showing that it has nothing to hide. You can be as altruistic as Mother Teresa, but if the public fails to buy that image, nothing matters. Do the right thing, communicate adeptly with the public via the news media, and your image problems will disappear.

Here are a few more points to keep in mind.

Do you know what body language makes you look like a liar on camera? Perfectly innocent things can trip you up. Squinting, even in sunlight. Throat clearing. Sweating. Touching the face. Use of "weasel words." Passive-voice syntax in your responses. You must carefully prepare, learning to banish ineffective body language from your behavioral repertoire, craft plain-language messages and project the appropriate emotional tone.

Be patient with the reporting and editing process. In virtually all media, whether electronic or print, reporters return from the field to the newsroom, where they must face an editor who will review their work meticulously, looking for holes and thinking up any questions the writing brings to mind. The editor is likely to ask several questions, trying to punch holes in the story, on the lookout for inconsistencies or ambiguities. The editor is not trying to torture the reporter or the reporter's sources. He or she is simply trying to anticipate how readers will react to the story. Ambiguity must be eliminated, clarity ensured, before the presses roll.

The reporter must have ready answers to each of the editors' questions, which means that he or she will gather much more information during the reporting process than is actually needed for the story. The editors' questions may result in revisions to the story and/or the reporter getting back in touch with you for more detail or with new questions. Looking good to his or her editor, as well as to competing news professionals, is extremely important to the reporter. One of the worst things that can happen in a newsroom is for a reporter to get something wrong.

That being said, even with everyone operating in good faith, the nature of news is such that drama is emphasized from the opening sentence onward, and sometimes a white-hat, black-hat dichotomy is central to painting the conflict that is at the heart of every news story.

If a news reporter has asked you or your organization a question, by all means answer it ASAP. Do you want to be the source for information about your company? Or do you want your competition, critics and adversaries to hold that position of privilege? The reporter may well quote those people anyway, but far better for you to frame the issues, to take the opportunity to reinforce key messages, to show yourself as accessible and open.

Letting others tell your story invites misinformation about your company to infiltrate the media, becoming part of the information archives that other journalists in the future will consult and may repeat verbatim when writing about you in the future.

You cannot control what a news reporter can learn from sources other than yourself. You can only position yourself as the source to be trusted, the one who understands the reporter's mission to dig out the truth.

The best media-relations practice is to be proactive in advance of predictable deadline situations. Don't wait for your industry or your company to become page 1-A material before you start cultivating reporters on the beat. Invite local reporters in periodically for updates. Keep in touch with national reporters via phone if you work for an industry that earns media coverage. Make sure they understand you are accessible and committed to getting them accurate information, fast. The reporter on your doorstep in times of crisis will have already generated his or her own perceptions of your company and will come to you wondering—even while anticipating—how you may react.

A final note: never try to squelch the conflict. If you want a story to go away, if you are bent on avoiding negative news coverage, you might think, "The best strategy is to downplay any conflict." A story of low conflict won't get much play, or so the reasoning goes. Not! Reporters are trained to sniff out conflict. There is always a conflict. If you haven't identified it in your particular case, you haven't thought the situation through. And if you attempt to downplay the conflict, reporters will turn their suspicions on you. They will wonder why you are so eager to keep this story out of the news.

Checklist for mobilizing during a crisis

- assemble the communications team

- seek your lawyer's advice on what should and should not be put in writing

- set up times for the team to meet informally during the day via conference calls or "dark" Web sites

- decide whether a proactive or reactive response strategy to the media best serves your organization

- assign a member of the team to immediately begin drafting key messages

- when using e-mail on the subject of the crisis, address all communications to your lawyer and cc: all other parties to better make the case that the communication is "privileged"

- keep the team's focus on researching stories and anecdotes that reinforce the bottom line of what you most want the public to understand

- make sure everyone in your organization knows to refer any calls from the news media to the communications team

- hire a media-relations consultant if the stakes are high

CHAPTER ELEVEN

LEVERAGING THE INTERNET

CHAPTER 11:
Leveraging the Internet

It seems like technology is taking over our world. Cell phones and computers are quickly becoming smaller. You hear non-stop talk about the new iPod or iPhone. CDs are quickly becoming a thing of the past, replaced by MP3s. Phone calls are being replaced by text messaging. Technological change is everywhere, and this is most evident in the fact that more and more people are connected to the Internet.

The Internet fundamentally changed the world of the news media. Information overload is a given as consumers switch among myriad channels and choices. No longer does a single mention in print or one soundbite on TV suffice to create a memorable impression. As you select a publicity vehicle of choice, you must decide not just among radio, TV and web, but also among the Internet's many venues including podcasts, YouTube videos, blogs and live chats.

To be sure, the Internet is not the be-all and end-all. No better substitute exists to establish credibility than being quoted in a prestigious print publication or writing an article for one. At the same time, a look at the world of marketing shows advertising dollars pouring into cyber media. Some $3 billion is spent in the United States annually on e-mail marketing, according to the EmailInsider.

And Americans conduct *more than 10 billion* Internet searches a month, extrapolating from January 2008 figures collected by the measurement firm comScore.

The nation's top five online news sites in the print newspaper and magazine category are *The New York Times, People Magazine, The Washington Post, TV Guide* and *USA Today*, according to a Hitwise analysis of 10 million users (February 2008).

Documenting the shift of consumers from traditional news outlets to the web, a Zogby Interactive nationwide survey (February 2008) found that almost half of Americans get their news primarily from the Internet. The 48 percent who indicate an Internet preference are up from 40 percent who gave that answer the year before. And when you look at younger adults (ages 18 to 29), the number jumps to 55 percent. The only age group to favor a primary news source other than the Internet is the nation's oldest—those 65 and up.

Interestingly, almost two-thirds (59 percent) of respondents see blogging as significant in journalism's future. This response demonstrates the success of the blog as a news and opinion vehicle—highly personal compared with traditional news genres.

While print media is still the most powerful source of publicity, it's important to supplement it with an Internet presence. Think about it: Many Americans spend their work hours in front of a computer surfing the Internet about topics they are interested in. That's the perfect time for them to be looking at your blog or Web site and hearing your message. The Internet also makes your message readily available for people to see all around the world. That's a lot of people who could be listening to what you are saying.

Trick of the trade: Take advantage of the new category "citizen journalist." No matter where you live, your local newspaper is likely to be reaching out for fresh voices to boost its online presence. Check the radio and TV station online news sites as well. Sometimes opportunities arise when a big story breaks in your city. In offering a journalistic piece to the editors and the public, you may reap valuable exposure. Remember: Reporting as a citizen journalist, your reputation is on the line. So check and recheck your facts and the spelling of all names, just as a "real" reporter would.

Understand the speed of the medium. Be prepared for quick action or reaction whether you are posting a video to YouTube or, God forbid, responding to a swirl of negative publicity. Case in point: The so-called "death-by-Twitter" of Sarah Lacy during her interview with Facebook's Mark Zuckerberg. What happened to Sarah Lacy could only have occurred in this new Internet era.

A company called SXSW Interactive invited Lacy, who writes the "ValleyGirl" column for *BusinessWeek*, to do the interview with the sought-after Facebook founder. In front of a live audience of convention-goers, the episode ended terribly. Lacy nattered on and on, crossed her legs, leaned flirtatiously toward Zuckerberg and somehow made the interview all about her.

The live audience protested with hoots, laughter and asides. "But here's where the Zuckerberg/Lacy interview differs from the usual lousy conference Q&A," according to the *Social Media Insider* online newsletter. "Those in attendance

151

began to criticize her, in real-time, on Twitter, blogs and in the real world, bringing a brand new meaning to the term 'mobisode,' which used to mean a small, portable episode of a TV show... At one point, when Zuckerberg offered that maybe Lacy should ask questions [instead of talking about herself], the crowd cheered for 30 seconds that seemed like five minutes, and somehow, between the Twitter postings, the news stories, the posting of the interview on YouTube, and so on, Sarah Lacy found herself in the middle of a Web 2.0 perfect storm—which has continued to feed on social media's power. Now that's a mobisode!"

Start reading blogs. Blogging is all about sharing a wealth of knowledge. Anyone who has a computer and an interest in your subject can search online and find blogs. There are blogs about almost everything you can think of. Read them. Utilize them. Leave comments and feedback for other authors. By becoming active in the blogging community, others will see that you are serious about your topic and about gathering useful information. Reading a lot of blogs will also show you which authors know their topics well, as opposed to those who are blogging just for the heck of it.

Write your own blog. The blog is quickly becoming one of the most powerful sources of publicity that you can have. It's a chance for you to convey your message while keeping the tone relaxed and casual. Readers also have an easy medium to connect with you by leaving comments on specific posts. Blogs are also a great asset because they can be updated quickly from almost anywhere. A great blog is one that gives quality information while giving the readers the impression that they know you and can talk to you about anything.

Reach out to the blogging community. Bloggers are a great asset when trying to gain publicity. Don't be afraid to take the initiative and reach out to them. If you find a blog you like, research it and find the contact information. Then send the writer an e-mail telling him or her why you like the blog and what separates it from blogs that cover the same topic. Also, don't be afraid to ask them if they have any tips to help your blog in the right direction. You'll be surprised how willing most of them are to help you out.

Promote your "home base." Many people don't realize how powerful a tool their Web sites can be. Many people have one simply because of the "peer-pressure" factor of being on the Internet. When it comes to Internet publicity, having a great Web site is the most important thing you can do. It's a place where people can learn all about you or your company, order products or just get in touch with you. Once you've taken the time to put together a great website, show it off. Put your website URL on everything: business cards, TV commercials, radio spots, e-mail signatures and anything else that people are going to hear or see.

Do your research. Depending on the nature of your business or the subject matter of your expertise, you may find surprising promotional vehicles on the Internet. For instance, musician David Samuel, writing on helium.com, shares with the musician community a list of "very good sites that will assist in promoting your band. I am on over one hundred sites and closing in on two hundred." Samuel's list:

www.garageband.com
www.indiebible.com

www.soundclick.com
www.sonicbids.com
www.purevolume.com
www.musicnation.com
www.musicsubmit.com
www.unsigned.com
www.facebook.com
www.mog.com
www.download.com

For those ready to embrace the digital movement, the rewards Internet publicity can garner are gigantic. Remember, the best publicity doesn't always come from a big corporate office in the middle of a metropolis. Sometimes you just have to roll up your sleeves and reach out on your own. The Internet is the easiest and most effective means of doing this, and the potential is out there for your name to be spread to every corner of the globe. Isn't that what you were hoping for in the first place?

Assuming that your Web site is up and running and your blog is humming along, here is a checklist to see whether you've overlooked any other valuable Internet communication vehicles:

- **E-zine.** You can create an online newsletter and distribute it to your e-mail list. Create content based on your area of expertise or simply offer a consumer-oriented list of tips related to your service or business. Define your target market, and make sure your material adds value to their lives. (And make sure your subscribers agree to receive your e-zine, or you might be classified as a spammer.)

- **RSS.** Short for Really Simple Syndication, RSS is a way for consumers to automatically receive new ongoing content, such as posts from your blog or summaries of all of your new content or podcasts. You can also use RSS feeds from other sites to refresh the content of your site with current news and developments.

- **Podcast.** You can create a following of listeners for your "radio show" by distributing it as an MP3 file. Consumers can then tune in on their iPods (hence the name podcast) or other digital players and/or personal computers. You can record a podcast using your computer, relatively inexpensive software and a microphone.

- **Multimedia promotion.** Employ not just text but also audio and video on your website to promote yourself or your business or service. Consider streaming audio with a message or perhaps an excerpt from a book or article you've written. When audio streams, it downloads as the listener listens—no waiting for a big file to move. Don't make your audio automatic; this irritates people. Let them choose to listen to your message by clicking a button.

- **Online media kits.** Include everything you might in a print media kit—news releases, a headshot, magazine articles about you, a list of suggested story ideas. An online kit carries an advantage over the print kit—here you can post soundbites from video and radio interviews. Two things to consider in creating online press releases: the general public as well as journalists may read them, and you may want to make sure your target keywords are well represented in the headline and body of the release.

ABOUT THE AUTHOR
Pam Lontos

Pam Lontos is founder and president of PR/PR, a public relations firm based in Orlando, Fla. Her company specializes in representing experts, authors and speakers at all levels. Pam has earned the Certified Speaking Professional (CSP) designation by the National Speakers Association and chairs their Writers and Publishers Professional Experts Group. She is also the former Vice President of Sales for Disney's Shamrock Broadcasting, in charge of eight radio stations, two TV stations and a production company. Pam is also the author of *Don't Tell Me It's Impossible Until After I've Already Done It* (William Morrow & Company).

With her years of experience in promotion, along with a master's degree in advertising and psychology, Pam knows the publicity ropes. She and her dedicated team of publicity agents at PR/PR have placed clients in publications such as *USA Today, The Wall Street Journal, Entrepreneur, Real Simple, Time Magazine, Investor's Business Daily, Reader's Digest, Cosmopolitan* and *U.S. News & World Report*. Clients have also appeared on numerous Internet sites, television shows and in association and trade journals. PR/PR's publicity services include a combination of print, Internet and television packages.

Some of PR/PR's clients include Brian Tracy (author of 40 books), Oscar- and Emmy- nominee Diane Ladd, LeAnn Thieman (author of *Chicken Soup for the Nurse's Soul, Second Dose*), Jason Jennings (author of *Less is More*), and Sy Sperling (founder of Hair Club for Men). The firm also works with professionals who are just launching their companies, books or careers.

- For a free publicity consultation, e-mail Pam@prpr. net or call 407-299-6128.

- To receive free publicity tips today, go to www. PRPR.net and register for our monthly e-newsletter, PR/PR Pulse!

- For additional CDs, articles and products to get you more publicity, e-mail Pam@prpr.net or call 407-299-6128.

ABOUT THE AUTHOR
Andrea Brunais

Experienced in both PR and journalism, Andrea Brunais has media trained doctors, scientists, authors and business professionals. She has handled media relations for major institutions such as the H. Lee Moffitt Cancer Center & Research Institute in Tampa, Fla., and the Robert C. Byrd Health Sciences Center at West Virginia University in Morgantown. At Moffitt Cancer Center, she helped increase positive news coverage by more than 250 percent annually.

Named Outstanding Graduate in Journalism by the faculty at the University of South Florida, Andrea's award-winning career includes senior writing and editing positions at Knight Ridder and Media General newspapers. Early in her career, she won a Robert Kennedy Journalism Award followed by first-place writing awards recognizing her coverage of topics such as medicine, law, education and the environment.

For more intensive study of some of the topics included in this book, please see her list of affordable training CDs and DVDs at *ink-inc.tv*

Audio CD titles include *Reach New Markets With Publicity*, an interview offering practical tips on how to increase your business by generating positive news coverage; and *Be Your Own Publicist*, with Andrea's coaching on ways to increase publicity that positions you as an expert. The DVD *Publicity Secrets from Inside the News Media* features a 40-minute excerpt from actual media training of a Sierra Club group and includes an 8-page reference manual.

- To add the CDs or DVDs to your learning library, email: Andrea@ink-inc.tv or call 304-920-5003.

- Mention *I See Your Name Everywhere* for a 20 percent discount off the DVD *Publicity Secrets from Inside the News Media*.

****

SPECIAL OFFER!

$219 worth of PR secrets are waiting for you. It's our special gift to you just for buying this book.

Here's what you'll get:

- A free powerful audio download package by Pam Lontos that will guide you through the essentials of *Finding Your Unique Hook*. You'll tailor your message for the media, get into magazines and newspapers and onto television and radio shows.

- A free download of the *Hook Questionnaire*. Use this information to create your unique hook, grab the media's attention and get booked or interviewed.

- A free How-to Article Guide packed with expert tips on how to create a unique how-to article on any subject that the media will love. You'll also receive a free article-writing template that will make writing articles a snap.

- A free audio download by Pam Lontos on how to write articles that magazines will publish.

Get ready to put these secrets to work for you!
Visit us at www.prpr.net
to get your bonus package today!

****